FOLKLORE OF ENGLAND: 2

CUSTOMS IN YORKSHIRE

TONY FOXWORTHY

COUNTRY BOOKS

Published by Country Books
Courtyard Cottage, Little Longstone, Bakewell, Derbyshire DE45 1NN
Tel: 01629 640670
e-mail: dickrichardson@country-books.co.uk

ISBN 978-1-906789-17-6

© 2009 Tony Foxworthy

Front Cover:
Cheese Cake Gatherers, circa 1900-1905

A catalogue of titles published by Country Books and Ashridge Press
is available upon request.

CONTENTS

JULY

AUGUST

SEPTEMBER

ACKNOWLEDGEMENTS

I would like to explain to the reader that I do not rely on other books dealing with folklore, customs, etc. My research is done through local libraries (newspaper cuttings); from the people who take part in the custom; by writing, telephoning or more importantly, by visiting the custom itself and witnessing what takes place.

A big thank you to:
The Yorkshire Library Service for their great help
Janet Barclay for her wonderful typing and deciphering my dreadful handwriting
Brenda Godrich for her proof-reading of the book. I do not know what I would have done without her help!
A special thank you to Tommy Chambers of Norton-on-Tess for use of his photographs, in particular the Maypoles.

Tony Foxworthy
2009

JANUARY

SCRAMBLING FOR PENNIES AT DRIFFIELD

This is a custom just for children, usually between five and fifteen years. According to the local people, this custom dates back to the 1700's, but there is no evidence to substantiate this. It could be related to the travelling salesmen who would at one time set up at the end of the town, and to attract the town's people to come and buy from them, they would throw small items in the crowd, in the hope that they would stay and spend money.

The children of Driffield chant while walking down the main street:

> Here we are at oor toon end
> A shoulder o' mutton and a croon to spend
> Are we downhearted? No
> Will we win? Yes.

When the shopkeepers hear this they are ready to throw among the assembled children coins and small gifts like sweets, lollies, etc., and so they carry on walking down the street and each shop will throw their prizes.

This custom used to be held on New Year's Day, but since this is now a holiday and the shops, of course, are closed, the custom now happens on the first working day in the New Year.

There are two or three places in England that have a similar custom, but it usually involves the Mayor or Clerk to the Council throwing coins from the steps of the Town Hall. Driffield is unique because the children are moving along, and not just coins are thrown, and different people are throwing the items.

This is a very good custom, and the nice thing is that all the Driffield adults from parents, grandparents and great grandparents all took part at one time.

THE MERCHANT ADVENTURERS, YORK

The Guild of Merchant Adventurers of the City of York originally was a socio-religious organisation, and the minutes of the meetings date back to the 1420's.

The City Guild ran the export and import business of the city, the main trade being cloth. Merchants sailed to Holland and Germany with cargoes of cloth, wool and lead, and brought back corn and linen.

In 1430 the Merchants and Mercers received a Charter from Henry VI enabling them to openly finance and run a hospital (which in fact they had been running for some time before). The Merchant Adventurers of York played a most important part in the development of trade in Yorkshire, also protecting Yorkshire members from interference from London Adventurers.

There are two very interesting occasions that the Guild keeps alive, which are two wills that have been granted to the Adventurers. Thomas Herbert's will dated 14th January 1644 gave £30 to the end that there shall be a Sermon preached every Michaelmas Court, that the parson be paid 20 shillings (£1) and 10 shillings (50p) to be given to the poor women in the Hospital, if there is no sermon the whole to be divided amongst the poor women.

The 20 shillings was still paid to the parson until very recently, when a special coin was presented to the parson. After the service there is a "Goose Feast" held at the Adventurers Hall.

Since 1692, under the terms of the will of Mistress Jane Stainton, the company attends a service held at All Saints' Church on the last Sunday in January, when the chaplain preaches the Jane Stainton Sermon reminding members of their "latter end", and that one guinea (£1.05) be paid to the poor of the parish.

FEBRUARY

FISHERMENS' REMEMBRANCE, BRIDLINGTON

The "Great Gale" of 12ᵗʰ February 1871, in which over 40 seamen lost their lives, included the crew of the lifeboat in Bridlington. A Memorial Service was held at the Priory linked to a charitable fund, for dependants of the fishermen of Bridlington.

When the charitable fund ceased to exist, the Seamen's Annual Service also stopped, and it was over twenty years before the service was revived. This service has now become an annual service attended by the lifeboat crew with their families, friends and supporters.

The Memorial is to remember those who lost their lives in the Great Gale who are laid to rest in the Priory Churchyard, and immediately following the service there is a short Act of Remembrance at the

Memorial to those who lost their lives.

In the early years the service was a great event, and the lifeboat was brought up to the church. This practice ceased as the boats became larger and far too heavy to move. In 1988 a new lifeboat came to Bridlington, and this was brought to the Priory for the Service. The local Vicar holds a service on the nearest Sunday to the 12th February for blessing the lifeboat.

MARCH

KIPLINGCOTE DERBY

On the third Thursday in March each year, come rain, hail, shine or snow, the Kiplingcote Derby is run.

Yorkshire men and women are well known for their love of horses and horse-racing. There is an unfortunate saying, "Shake a bridle over a Yorkshireman's grave and he'll get up and steal your mare." This has obviously been originated by people on the other side of the Pennines.

The interesting thing about the Kiplingcote Derby is that the horse that comes in second receives more money than the rider of the winner.

The Derby was started, according to tradition, in 1519, but it was not until 1619 that a number of local nobility, who wanted to see how well their horses had survived the winter months, invested £365 so that the

winner in those days would receive the interest on the investment each year. It is still the same today, in that the winner receives the interest, but the second prize is made up from all the entry fees that the riders pay so that they can compete in the oldest flat race in England (some say the world). Having said that the Derby started in 1519, the earliest records only go back to 1555.

The winner also receives a cup, which went missing during the 18th century; there never seemed enough money to buy another. In 1970 a new cup was donated by a Mrs Jean Mellonie in 1939, when she was just 19 years old, on her third attempt became the first woman to win the race. Sadly the cup only lasted for a few years. Now there is another trophy donated by Mrs Mellonie's daughter in memory of her mother.

The riders have to be weighed, and this is done at the finishing post. Riders must be ten stones, and if they are not, then stones are tied to the rider until they weigh in at ten stone. This is done between 10.30 am and 11.30 am.

The riders and horses assemble at the starting post, which is about a mile north of Kiplingcote railway station. They are off at 1 pm. The course is a very rough one. They cross a railway line and a major road and down and up muddy lanes for four and a half miles.

Remember the third Thursday in March.

MAY

MAY POLES

Quite a number of folklore authors state in their books that there are only four or five permanent May Poles still standing. It is obvious that these expert authors have done very little, if any, research on the May Pole, because there are 25 permanent May Poles still standing in Yorkshire alone.

The English May Pole in days gone by would have been found in practically every village, and it would have been danced around by the villagers in a hand-to-hand circle around the Pole, circling left, right and in and out, with maybe a grand chain, etc. The May Pole dance with little girls in white dresses using ribbons and making a pretty pattern was brought over to England from Europe.

Below is a list of the May Poles still standing in Yorkshire.

ALDBOROUGH – 45 feet high, wooden, with red, white and blue spirals.
APPLETON WISKE – 15 feet high, silver steel tube.
BARWICK IN ELMET – 89 feet (approximately), wooden. Every three years the Pole is taken down on Easter Monday, repainted, and on Spring Bank Holiday Tuesday is erected for another three years.
BURNSALL – 40 feet high, wooden, unpainted. The next village of Thorpe occasionally tries to steal the Pole.
CONISTONE – 45 feet high, wooden, unpainted.
CRAIKHALL – 12 - 15 feet high, wooden.
ELVINGTON – 20 feet high, wooden, white, red, white, blue sections. Raised for the Queen's Silver Jubilee in 1977.
GALPHAY – 40 feet high, wooden. Raised for George V's Silver Jubilee

in 1935, and in memory of Admiral Charles Oxley.

GAWTHORPE – 40 feet high, wooden. A grand celebration takes place, with a procession and feast. A May Queen is elected.

HUTTON LE HOLE – 20 feet high, wooden. Painted half white, upper half blue.

KETTLEWELL – 20 feet high, plastic tube, cream. Erected for Queen Elizabeth's Coronation, 1953.

LINTON IN CRAVEN – 35 - 40 feet high, wooden. Painted red and white.

LONG PRESTON – 25 feet high, wooden. Pole renewed around 1970.

NABURN – 25 feet high, fibreglass. New Pole erected for Queen Elizabeth's Coronation, 1953.

NUN MONKTON – 88 feet high, the tallest Pole in England. Wooden. White and green spirals.

OTLEY – There are two Poles in Otiey side by side. The taller one is 60 feet high, the other 25 feet high. It is possible that a Pole has stood here since the restoration of Charles II in 1660.

RAINTON – 15 feet high, wood. Painted white. Erected by the people of Rainton on the Royal Jubilee, 1977.

RUTHWELL – 20 feet high. Painted white with red and blue slim stripes. Paid for with the profits of a successful Carnival.

ROXBY – 65 feet high, wooden.

SINNINGTON – A steel Pole. Locals report that there has been a Pole in Sinnington since the 1600s.

SLINGSBY – Over 10 feet high, claims to have been a May Pole since 1799.

UPPER POPPLETON – 64 feet high, white with red and blue spirals. Erected for the National Celebrations for Queen Elizabeth Il's Jubilee, 1977.

WADWORTH – 35 feet high, steel tube. Blue, white, red and black vertical sections. Brand new Pole erected in 1996.

WETHERBY – 50 feet high, wooden. Not painted, except for white vertical stripes.

EARSWICK AND WHIXLEY – In a new estate built around a village green, as though they are old villages.

Earswick – 15 feet high, wooden. Painted red, white and blue.

Whixley – 15 feet high, wooden. Green spirals on white.

Aldborough   *Appleton Wiske*

Barwick in Elmet   *Burnsal*

19

Conistone

Craikhall

Galphay

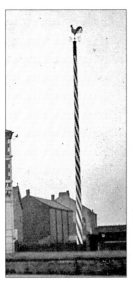

Gawthorpe

Hutton le Hole

Kettlewell

 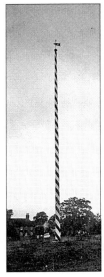 

Linton in Craven   *Nun Monkton*   *Long Preston*

Otley   *Rainton*   *Ruthwell*

Sinnington

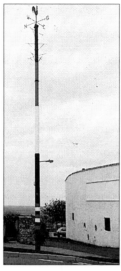

Wadworth

Upper Poppleton

Whixley

Earswick

Levisham

Slingsby

Whixley

THE ANTIENT SCORTON SILVER ARROW, SCORTON

The Scorton Arrow is a contest for archers, and the pedigree can be traced back for an absolute certainty to 14th May 1673. There were 22 archers competing on the village green of Scorton, which is near Richmond, North Yorkshire. The winner on this occasion was a Henry Carlverley.

You can imagine the 22 archers after the contest all sitting around discussing the day's activities, when someone happened to say wouldn't it be a good idea to hold this event every year, and that is what has happened. The Antient Scorton Silver Arrow Contest has been held each year since 1673.

The first Champion, Henry Carlverley, was automatically elected Captain, and according to the rules was able to suggest where the next contest would take place. It must be in Yorkshire, but not necessarily in Scorton.

Again at the very first meeting some rules were drawn up, one of which was a ruling about swearing. The swear bag is always available at each meeting. What warrants a "swear" nowadays? There are certain words that are not swearing, whereas in 1673 swearing was a different kettle of fish.

There have been very few breaks in the contest, one noticeably when there was a long hiatus between the 1790's and 1809, but only pestilence and World Wars have been allowed to break the sequence.

The Silver Arrow is a priceless trophy and is well looked after by the archers. It was broken once by an undergraduate from Oxford who used the Silver Arrow in 1760, and when he shot it it was damaged, but it was soon repaired. According to the Assay Master, the tail of the arrow is sixteenth century and the fore part seventeenth century silver.

Legend has it that the Silver Arrow was presented to the club by

Queen Elizabeth I. It seems that Roger Ascharn, who taught the Queen archery, was a regular at the Scorton contest. He lived at nearby Kirby Wiske, and he is supposed to have persuaded the Queen to present the arrow to the club.

The winner of the Silver Arrow is the first archer that strikes an inner gold at one hundred yards, and he immediately becomes the Captain for the next twelve months. He has to choose the next venue within the 1974 boundaries of Yorkshire, but his main responsibility is the organising of the next Silver Arrow Contest.

There are other trophies presented throughout the day. The runner-up is made Lieutenant, and his trophy is an elegant bugle which he has to blow (with all sorts of different sounds), to signal the commence-ment of the next meeting. Another trophy is the Horn Spoon lined with silver, which bears the warning, in Latin, "Don't laugh at me, my friends". There is no need to laugh at him, because the winner also receives all the money left at the end of the day's shooting. Another trophy is the Wilkinson Sword, donated by Wilkinsons the cutlers. The Sword is also known as the Ben Hird Trophy. It commemorates one of the best loved of the Scorton veterans who died in 1976.

There are other trophies. The Thirsk Insignia was given to the society by the Thirsk Bowmen in 1884. This competition is restricted to Yorkshiremen only. Then there is the Arrow, the Belt and Quiver won by the highest scorer, a Bugle which is awarded for the highest number of hits, and a silver medal going to the best gold, who receives half the money collected at the meeting. There are a couple of other perks. If you score a gold you are rewarded with two shillings, and if you score any other colour you are rewarded with one shilling. Anyone who scores a white has to put one shilling in the kitty. If you miss the target completely there is no award or forfeit. Missing the target is bad enough.

The contest takes place in May or June. The Lieutenant sounds the bugle at 10.30am, when the contest starts. At 1pm lunch is served, and it restarts at 3.30pm, finishing at 5.30pm.

WALKING THE BOUNDARY, TODMORDEN

Although this event is only 26 years old, having been started in 1982 and organised by the Rotary and the Inner Wheel, the walkers are in fact enacting a very old custom that dates back to pre-Christian days, when the whole village or town would walk or ride the boundaries, and each boundary mark would be beaten with willow wands, sticks, etc., and it was called Beating the Bounds.

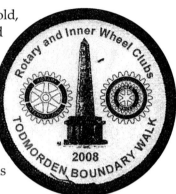

The Walkers of Todmorden all gather on the Sunday of the first May Bank Holiday, which means it can fall any time between 30th April and 6th May. The walk is about 22 miles venturing round the outskirts of Todmorden.

In 2008 the committee introduced another walk, known as the Pike Hike, which is a shorter walk of a mere twelve miles for the less hardy people. In the early days of the walk it attracted 100-150 walkers, and in its heyday 500 to 550 people attended. Then the custom stopped for three years because of Foot and Mouth

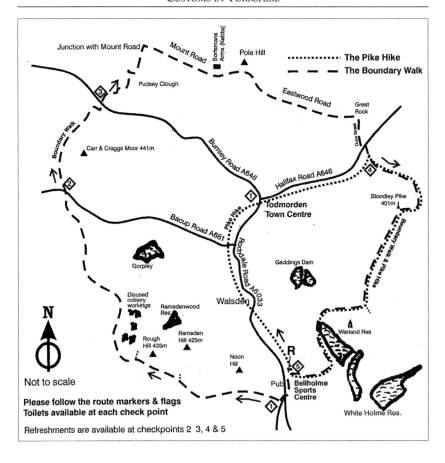

Disease, which has lowered the numbers to about 250. Even so, the whole day is enjoyed by everyone, and in particular the charity that the committee has chosen, who benefit by quite a substantial amount.

JUNE

BARNABY FAIR, BOROUGHBRIDGE

BARNABY BRIGHT – LONGEST DAY AND SHORTEST NIGHT

This Horse Fair was once a thriving Fair, because the main road was used to show off the horses by running up and down that road. It was so dangerous that everyone living on the main road boarded up their windows, etc., so that nothing got broken.

The fair used to be held on the Old St Bartholomew's Day (22nd June) and lasted for three weeks, but it is now held on the Tuesday nearest to 22nd June.

Barnaby Fair was not the only fair in Boroughbridge. There was on, 27th and 28th April, a fair for horned cattle and sheep, then there was a week in June that saw hardware, cloth and small goods, and 25th and 26th October for sheep and cattle.

Barnaby Fair was a great fair in its time, and people came from miles around, not just visitors but traders, etc. In the weeks before the fair, great preparations were made for the traders by the erection of booths, stalls and tents. The common ground and the fields just outside of the town saw people of all descriptions – Gypsies, hawkers, tinkers, fortune-tellers, horse copers and ragamuffins. A special sort of light vessels, known as Barnaby boats, came up the river with goods and merchandise for the fair, and the amount of trade done was enormous.

There was a curious custom here, provided by Charter of 1622, which permitted any householder of Boroughbridge to sell liquor on the two principal days of the fair, being the 22nd and 23rd June. Liquor so sold might be consumed on or off the premises. Many of the householders availed themselves of the privilege of the Charter to erect a tent or a booth outside their houses wherein the customers might be accommodated. The hanging of a bush above the front door showed that liquor was available. Lemon curd tarts were baked, and they were known as Barnaby tarts, which were sold to any passer-by.

The fair today is nothing like the old days. Very few horses are bought and sold, not many trades are visible, in fact it has lost a great deal of its character, and it is whispered around that the locals want to stop the fair. Pity.

HEPWORTH FEAST

The village name is taken from the Anglo-Saxon "Hep" signifying high, and "worth", a residence. So we have a place of high residence, with Hepworth being on high ground and maybe considered as answering pretty correctly to this description.

The plague visited Hepworth around the same time as it was ravaging London City in 1665. It seems that a quantity of clothing was sent to Foster Place (a farmhouse near Hepworth), then occupied by a family of the name of Beover. It is said that the cloth was sent by a relative in London who died of the plague. After its arrival, those who unpacked the parcel fell ill and shortly afterwards died, and those who helped the family also fell ill and died. Through this passing on to individuals it eventually reached Hepworth, the southern part of the village, where it appears to have raged with considerable violence. As the plague spread, the inhabitants of the north-west part of the village had not as yet been visited by it. They decided to cut themselves off from their neighbours. They built a large fence across the main road, and refused to communicate with anyone on the other side of the fence. This meant that this part of the village did not catch the dreaded disease.

It is believed that the Hepworth feast is a celebration to remember those who died from the plague and those who escaped. On the other hand, it has been suggested that it could be the remnants of a pagan Midsummer Festival, seeing that the present day festivities take place on the last Monday in June

The celebration today starts at 2 pm with a procession through the village, consisting usually of schoolchildren (the school is closed on this day). The procession is led by the Hepworth band. Starting from the junior school, they process through the village, pay a visit to the

village of Scholes and come back up the hill to Hepworth. At intervals en route the procession will stop and sing a hymn. On returning to the village, a free tea is available in the school. After the tea there are sports for the children.

At one time there were two bands, the Hepworth Band and the Hepworth Iron Company Band, but with the Iron Company's demise only Hepworth Band remains. The day finishes with the village band and the gathering of the crowds outside the Butchers Arms where everyone joins in a united sing.

CHURCH YCLEPPING, TANKERSLEY

The church is dedicated to St. Peter, and St. Peter's Church is in the Diocese of Sheffield, so it is interesting that such a custom has survived in a village that has become part of the City of Sheffield.

Yclepping is taken from the old English word "clypping", to embrace, and it is more commonly known as clipping.

Tankersley clipping takes place on the second Sunday following June 29th (St. Peter's Day) when the clergy, choir and congregation process to the outside of the church and all hold hands in a big circle around the church, embracing the building. It seems that at one time they had a bugle player on the top of the church tower who would play the hymn tune and the "clippers" would all sing.

It is believed that the custom is very old, in fact pre-Christian, but there is no evidence that this is so, except that the pre-Christians at certain special times, like May 1st, would sacrifice a goat or other small animal and then they would join hands in a circle and sing and dance round the sacrificial altar. So the church clipping could be related to that.

The clipping of St. Peter's Church at Tankersley only goes back as far as the 1920s when the then incumbent introduced the custom to the then congregation. It seems that at one point the clipping didn't take place, but it was revived in the 1970's and has continued with much enthusiasm by the people of Tankersley.

Tankersley Church is built on the foundations of an earlier place of worship which goes back to Saxon and almost certainly pre-Christian times.

Out of interest, there is a mention of a Rector and church in Tankersley in the Domesday Book.

Another little custom which takes place on Clipping Day is the

presentation of the Fenn Bibles. These Bibles are presented to the children who are best versed in Biblical knowledge, in memory of the Rev. William Mason Fenn.

Well Dressing in South Yorkshire

Those people who know something of English Customs will know that Well Dressings are found mainly in the county of Derbyshire. Up until a few years ago the only Well Dressings were in Derbyshire (but for one in Staffordshire.

Now Well Dressings can be found in Leicestershire, Nottinghamshire, Greater Manchester, Cheshire, Staffordshire, Shropshire, Somerset, and of course, South Yorkshire.

The Dressing is usually a picture depicting a story from the Bible, and the picture is made up of petals, flowers, grass, leaves etc, anything from the soil. The picture is made on a large board with a frame, and these are placed in the local river, pond, etc. and left there for a few days. The dressers then make a clay that is spread on to the board and frame, and the picture is scratched on to the clay, and then the petals, flowers, etc, are laid on the clay making usually a religious picture.

The reason why South Yorkshire has so many Dressings is because some years ago the government rearranged the boundaries of some counties. South Yorkshire embraced North Derbyshire, therefore bringing Well Dressings to Yorkshire.

CONISBOROUGH – had a Well Dressing for the Millennium in 2000. They included the Blessing of the Well with their Harvest Festival.
DORE – The Dressings are erected on the first Saturday in July. There are two wells dressed, Village Green Well and Guide Well. The Dressing coincides with the village Flower Festival. The Dressings are blessed eight days later.
HARTHILL – The Dressings are erected on the second Monday in July and blessed on the same day.
HOPE – There are four Wells dressed at Hope on a Sunday around St.

Hope

Peter's Day (29th June), and blessed on the same day.

MIDHOPESTONE – Two Dressings are erected sometime in June.

PENISTONE – Only one Well is dressed on the Second Sunday in June, and blessed on the same day.

WATH UPON DEARNE – A Dressing was erected here for the Millennium.

WICKERSLEY – A Dressing was erected for the Millennium by the Methodist Church.

Dore

THE FRIENDLY SOCIETY, ASKRIGG

Askrigg is a small village just north of Bainbridge in the North Riding. In the late 18th and 19th century when the so-called Industrial Revolution took place, it meant that it would change the lives of both town and country. It meant that a large number of people became redundant, particularly in the country.

The Poor Law Act was passed by the Government in 1601. Support was given to the local poor by giving money to help them, but this was taken from the ratepayers. This form of payment went well until 1800, when the poor increased very rapidly and the ratepayers were very reluctant to pay. The 1601 Act was no longer adequate, so the Act was no longer available. In 1834 the Poor Law Amendment Act established Poor Law Unions through the country and laid down the principle that poor relief would only be paid to the inmates of the Workhouse.

So it was time to organise some form of organisation to help people financially. Although many Friendly Societies were established during

Annual church service

Annual sports day

the 18th century, it was only from the 1790's, when the problem of poverty and the increased burden of poor relief became acute, that the number of Friendly Societies and their membership expanded rapidly. It was estimated that by 1800 there were over 7,000 Friendly Societies in England and Wales.

The Askrigg Friendly Society was formed in 1809 and is still going strong today. The full name of the Society is Askrigg Equitable, Benevolent and Friendly Society. The Society looks after the welfare of its members by giving sick pay when they are ill or are out of a job.

They meet four times a year, and once a year the Society parades through the village with their banners in the lead, processing to the church of St. Oswald. After the service they continue the procession to their headquarters in the Kings Arms Hotel, where they hold their AGM, followed by a slap-up meal.

The parade and sports are held some time in June.

JULY

CHURCH CLIPPING, GUISELEY

Guiseley is north-west of Leeds and south of Otley. The church is dedicated to St. Oswald, and the clipping takes place on the first Sunday in July, but it used to be held on August 5th.

The clipping is just part of a weekend Festival associated with the church. On the Saturday the clergy, choir and dignitaries all process from the church to the Cross in Towngate, where a service is held and the congregation is addressed by a top-ranking church dignitary.

The Sunday of that weekend sees the Clipping of the Church, when clergy, choir and congregation hold hands around the church, and they all raise their hands and shout three times "God Bless Our Church", to the general astonishment of passers-by.

BEATING THE BOUNDS, SPAINTON

Spainton is an isolated village near Pickering in North Yorkshire, and it has a Beating of the Bounds. It is another unusual Custom in that it only takes place usually years and years apart. The Boundary Walk is performed when a new Lord of the Manor inherits the large estate. The walk around the boundary by the new Lord is one of the first things that has to be done when taking over the estate. The boundary is 27 miles long, the same now as in Norman times.

It was last done on 14th - 15th July 1986, when the new Lord took over, but he was only 19 years old at the time, so it could still be a long time before the Bounds are Beaten again.

BLESSING THE BOATS, WHITBY

Whitby is on the north-east coast of Yorkshire, just north of Scarborough. It is a town that is split in two by the harbour. One side is the very old part with cobbled streets, etc., the other side being the holiday side with hotels and boarding houses, and where the summer entertainment takes place.

At one time the Blessing was to bless the herring fleet, but since 1946 there has been no herring fleet, because fishing for herring was banned. The Blessing now is for the fishing fleet.

A rather grand procession, which includes the clergy and choirs of all the Christian churches in Whitby, with the Bishop of Whitby in the lead, process to the harbour side, where the Bishop conducts a short service and then he blesses the fishing fleet. All the boats are on the opposite side of the harbour.

The ceremony takes place usually on the second Sunday in July at 2.30pm.

The custom is not very old, in fact it was started about 1954, but that doesn't mean that there has never been a blessing. It could, of course, be that some similar ceremony took place way back in medieval times.

THE STRAW RACE, OXENHOPE, NEAR KEIGHLEY

This race is like the World Coal Carrying Championship at Gawthorpe, although the Oxenhope Race has not yet reached world status.

At Oxenhope a team of two carries a bale of straw from just outside of the village and right through the village, and the route is such that the teams race past each of the village pubs. But like a number of races through the country, each team has to down a pint of beer at each pub, there being five pubs in all.

This very active custom only started in 1976, but because the whole village is involved and all taking part, it is a Custom.

Oxenhope is normally a very quiet village, but on a day in July each year, many thousands of visitors will flock into the village to see the Straw Race. There are over 400 competitors, each team consisting of two people, either two men or two women or a man and woman together.

The day is not just the Races but lots of other things take place like bouncy castles, brass bands, steel bands, parachute jumping, events for the children, and of course the pubs are open so there is a certain amount of drinking. Although all this is taking place, there has never been any trouble.

There is also a serious side to this custom, in that all the money collected from the racing teams goes to a local charity or charities. The teams also find sponsors for their run, so the charities do quite well. The money collected over past years has amounted to £250,000. All the competitors finish at the Dog and Gun where they all receive their finishing medal, a well-earned trophy of a most pleasant day.

Seamer Proclamation

An interesting part of the Fair, which sadly does not exist today, was that while the Fair was held at Seamer, people that brewed their own beer could open as a pub and sell their brew to the fairgoers. The way to prove that you were licensed for that time was to place a branch from a tree over the front door of the house.

Over the years Seamer Horse Fair has gone through great difficulties when the crowds were so large they could not be controlled, or on the other side not many people attending. Recently the Fair was cancelled because of Foot and Mouth disease.

Tommy Chambers

44

Seamer Charter
Proclamation

Whereas King Richard the Second, on the 11th of November, in the sixth year of his reign, in the year of our Lord, one thousand, three hundred and thirty seven, did grant unto the Lords of this Manor, and to their heirs for ever. One fair yearly to be kept in the said Manor, upon the fourth day of July, being St. Martin's Day (from the alteration in the style the fifteenth day of July) and so to continue for the space of seven days; by virtue of which grant and confirmation thereof from time to time.

We do openly proclaim, publish and declare, that this Fair, beginning on the fifteenth day of July and so for seven days following, except the Lord's day it shall and may be lawful for all and every person and persons resorting to this fair, to buy, sell, bargain or deal for any lawful Goods, Wares, Merchandise, Horses, Geldings, Mares, Colts, Fillies, Beasts, Sheep, or any other cattle whatsoever, paying unto the Lord of the Manor by his officers appointed to receive the same, Pollage, Package, Stallage, Standage, and other duties belonging to him for the same.

And we do in the Queen's Majesty's name straitly charge and command all manner of persons whatsoever coming and resorting to this Fair that they keep the Peace during this Fair and in the end so to depart.

God Save the Queen and the Lord of this Manor.

At the present time the crowds are coming to the Fair, with the Gypsies selling their horses, and in some cases dogs are sold as well. Also the streets are lined with stalls selling boots and shoes, trinkets, sweetmeats and, as the Charter says, "lawful goods, wares, merchandise, horses, geldings, mares, colts, fillies, beasts, sheep and any other cattle whatsoever."

Mind you, if the Horse Fair did not take place, the Charter would still be read by a man on horseback. Sometime in July.

KILBURN FEAST

Kilburn is a small village near Thirsk, North Yorkshire.

It is well known, for its hill end bears the figure of a white horse, a figure cut into the hillside in 1857. The name of the hill end is White Mare Crag or White Stone Cliff, and it is older than the carved figure. There are stories of a white horse ghost that parades around the area.

This custom lasts from the Saturday after 6th July.

The Sports takes place on the Saturday and Monday with all sorts of games and sports, the main event being a quoits match between the local villages. There is also a childrens' White Horse Fun Run.

The Tuesday sees the appearance of the Mock Mayor and Mayoress in their procession. The Mayor wears a top hat and dress suit, and the Mayoress is in her "posh" dress, bonnet, wig and heavy make-up, because this is a man dressed as a woman. The identity of the Mayoress is kept a secret until she appears with the "Mayor", who is the person that chooses the "Lady Mayoress". The "Mayor" and "Mayoress" go around the village as in a procession, on a decorated cart with a man, not a horse, pulling the cart. The procession goes round the village, stopping en route, fining the villagers for doing, or not doing, something like not drawing the house curtains, for not cutting the lawn, or for cutting the lawn, for leaving a gate open, etc. The fines take the shape of money, crisps, biscuits, drinks, etc. While all this is going on the "Lady Mayoress" is jumping from the cart to approach the women of the village to give them a very long

Tommy Chambers

46

and messy kiss, leaving rather large red lipstick marks on the surprised ladies.

The procession returns to the local pub, and the food, drink and money is used to make a feast for the "Mayor's" party.

At one time not so long ago, the Mayor's party, with the help of the villagers, sang a song known as "Old Grimy". According to some, "Old Grimy" was Grim, otherwise the Norse god Odin, but no definite conclusions can be made.

The song "Old Grimy" is below, just for your interest.

Old Grimy bought a load of bricks, to build his old chimney higher,
To keep his neighbours' cats and dogs from damping out the fire.

Chorus:
Old Grimy was a grand old chap, he's dead, he'll never die no more,
He used to wear a long frock coat buttoned down before.

Old Grimy bought a load of slabs, to slab his garden round
To keep his neighbours' cats and dogs from scratching up the ground.

Chorus:

Old Grimy had a little pig, and it was double-jointed,
He thought he'd make pork of it, but he was disappointed.

Chorus:

The squirrel is a pretty bird, it has a bushy tail
It used to be Old Grimy's corn...?

Chorus:

Why do those bugs torment me so, I never did them harm,
They come to me while I'm asleep, aye thousands in a swarm.

Chorus:

There was a bug among this lot, they called him big Joe,
He had two rows of double teeth upon his bottom jaw.

Chorus.

SEAMER HORSE FAIR

Seamer is a village just south of Scarborough. King Richard II granted the Charter for Seamer Fair to Henry Percy, Duke of Northumberland, giving authority for a market to be held at Seamer each Monday and for a Fair of a week's duration (excluding Sundays) to commence on the Feast of St. Martin, providing that it did not interfere with neighbouring markets and Fairs that had already been established (i.e. Scarborough, Brompton, Filey and Sherborne).

This Charter was given to the Lord of the Manor in 1383, although the Charter does state that it was granted in the sixth year of King Richard ll's reign in the year 1337. King Richard reigned from 1377 to 1399, so in the sixth year of his reign it should read 1383, but that date in the Charter stays, as you will see on page 45.

The original date for the Fair was July 4th, St. Martin's Day, but in 1752, when the Gregorian calendar was adopted, eleven days were added to the calendar; therefore today's Fair is proclaimed on July 15th.

The Charter is read out to all and sundry by a villager on horseback, the first reading being at 11am. To gain the attention of the people assembled, a crier shouts "Oyez, Oyez, Oyez".

The first Proclamation takes place on the village green, and then it is read in four other traditional places in the village. On the last reading the Lord or Lady of the Manor throw new pennies for the children to scramble for.

AUGUST

OLD GOOSEBERRY SHOW, EGTON BRIDGE, NEAR WHITBY

Growing gooseberries on a competitive basis seems to have started in Lancashire, Cheshire and the Midlands where the moist climate favoured gooseberries. The first Gooseberry Clubs were being formed around the Manchester area in the 1740's, where workers in the textile industry were particularly keen on developing new varieties of gooseberry, as well as growing ever larger specimens for their annual show.

The Egton Bridge Old Gooseberry Show was first started in 1800, making it the second oldest gooseberry show in England, the oldest

being Holmes Chapel in Cheshire. The show at Egton Bridge has been held every year since 1800 without a break.

The over a hundred members of the Gooseberry Club all know each other from their schooldays, likewise their fathers and grandfathers, so gooseberries are in the blood of the men of Egton Bridge. They live for the Annual Show. Gooseberries are the only fruit shown at the exhibition, and they reach mammoth proportions, the smallest being as big as a large plum. It is an unwritten rule that no-one will look at a neighbour's plant before the show takes place. The growers look after their gooseberries like royalty, with special treatment, covering the bush with netting so that the wasps don't get at them. The wasp is the main enemy of the gooseberry.

The children of the village try to get information from other growers' children, sometimes successfully but mostly without success. The show takes place on the first Tuesday of August each year. The judging starts at 9 am, and the public are allowed in at 3pm till 7pm. The gooseberries are weighed, and it is the heaviest in each class that wins.

The classes are for different varieties, as follows:

Careless
Lancer
Langley Cage
Laxton Amber
Leveller
May Doice
New Grant
Whinhams Industry
Whitesmith

The competitors are mostly from Egton Bridge and surrounding villages etc., but they do come from further afield, as far away as Lincolnshire.

If anyone decides to visit Egton Bridge to see the famous large gooseberries, just a little advice: do not call them gooseberries, they are known locally as "Berries".

TRADITIONAL GOOSEBERRY RECIPES

GOOSEBERRY FOOL – Take the tops and stalks from a pound of green goose-berries, and boil them with three-quarters of a pound of sugar and a cupful of water. When quite soft press them through a coarse sieve, and mix with them, very gradually, a pint of milk, or cream, if a richer dish is required. Serve when cold. This old-fashioned dish is wholesome and inexpensive, and, when well-made, very agreeable. Time, about twenty minutes to boil the fruit. Sufficient for six or seven persons.

GOOSEBERRY CHARLOTTE – Pick the tops and stalks from a pound and a half of gooseberries; wash and drain them, and boil them with a pound and a half of loaf-sugar, until reduced to a pulp. Press them through a coarse sieve. Take half a dozen sponge-biscuits, cut than into thin slices, and line a plain round mould with them. Pour in the fruit, cover it with slices of spongecake, place cover and a weight on the top, and let it remain until well set. Turn it out before serving, and pour some good custard or nicely-flavowed cream round it. Thin slices of bread may be used instead of sponge-biscuit. Time, ten or twelve hours to set properly. Sufficient for five or six persons.

GOOSEBERRY CHEESE – Pick the tops and stalks from some rough red goose-berries, fully ripe. Bake them in a moderate oven till soft, then pulp them through a fine sieve. Let them boil very gently, and add, a little at a time, a quarter of a pound of loaf-sugar to every pound of fruit-pulp. Boil, skim, and stir it for half an hour, then pour it on small plates, and dry it before the fire, or in a cool oven. When dry, keep the cheese between folds of white paper. Time, half an hour to boil.

GOOSEBERRY DUMPLING – Line a plain round basin or mould with a good suet crust. Pick the tops and stalks from as many gooseberries as will fill it, strew some moist sugar over the top, and cover with the paste. Pinch in the sides securely, to prevent the juice escaping, and tie in a floured cloth. Plunge the pudding into boiled water, and boil for two or three hours, according to the size of the pudding, Sufficient for six or seven persons.

FESTIVAL OF ST. OSWALD, GUISELEY

St. Oswald was the second Christian King of Northumbria, 634 to 642. Brought up at the Monastery of Iona, he invited St. Aidan to teach the faith to his people, and together they travelled over the Northern moors, the King translating the message of the missionary. St. Oswald was an effective King, for he maintained peace amongst his subjects. He was killed at Maserfield (near to Oswestry or Oswald's Tree) while fighting Penda, King of Mercia. St. Oswald is buried in Durham Cathedral.

The parish church of Guiseley is dedicated to St. Oswald, and his feast day is 9th August.

The Festival takes the form of a church service with a local Bishop and a Peer of the Realm being invited to take part by giving a sermon or holding a Public Meeting. The Church service is held, and, after the Blessing, the dignitaries lead the procession of the congregation,

singing a hymn as they process to the Cross in the middle of town. This is where the public meeting takes place. The singing of another hymn sees the procession proceed to the Town Hall, were tea is made available to all those attending.

The dignitaries, other than the Bishop and Peer, are the local Chairmen of the Councils of Ilkley, Otley, Baildon and Horsforth, all in full ceremonial costume. The procession also has the local church choir and clergy, so it makes a very spectacular procession moving through the town of Guiseley.

SCARECROW FESTIVAL, KETTLEWELL

The event is not a custom as such, as it only started in 1994, but if it continues for a number of years in the future it will most certainly become a custom. It has the major ingredient, in that the whole village is deeply involved.

The Festival started in 1994 as a fund-raiser for the local church. It was so successful that the Festival has continued, and in fact today there is a Scarecrow Festival Committee to see that the event is well run.

There are well over 100 scarecrows, and they can be found in the most prominent positions in the village, but there are a lot which can be found in hidden corners.

Some of the scarecrows are of well-known figures like the Disney characters, but there are also local people made into Scarecrows.

The Festival is attracting many thousands, and there is a scarecrow Trail for visitors to follow. Following this trail gives the visitor the opportunity to see this lovely picturesque village. The local tea rooms and village hall serve home-baked food.

At the present time the Festival is creating funds for St. Mary's Church, the Village Hall and the local school. The Festival is held around the second week of August.

THE FEAST OF ST. WILFRID, RIPON

St. Wilfrid was an English saint who lived in Saxon times. He became a monk at Lindsfarne and about AD605 was made Bishop of York. He had some disagreement with the Archbishop of Canterbury and left the country.

The Feast of St. Wilfrid, held on the first Saturday in August, commemorates Wilfrid's return from exile. The story goes that as St. Wilfrid was returning from exile in Rome, he was walking in England

towards Ripon, he fell dangerously ill and was very much just alive. For five days he was in this state. When he eventually awoke, he sat up in his bed and saw outside a large procession of many people singing and dancing and making a lot of noise. When he got back to Ripon he reflected on the vision he had seen, which he regarded as a promise of restoration and peace.

In the year 1108 King Henry I granted to the Archbishop of York the privilege of holding a Fair at Ripon at the Feast of St. Wilfrid, and the Fair has been held ever since.

There are two processions

on the first Saturday in August, the main one being St Wilfrid's Parade, with St. Wilfrid on a white horse led by a monk. St. Wilfrid is in full Bishop's robes. There are usually two bands like the local Ripon brass band. Following St. Wilfrid are quite a number of floats, and they each have a theme. This means that all the local groups – Boy Scouts, Young Farmers, St. John's Ambulance, the Rotary Club, etc., take part. Over the days that the festival takes place there are a number of activities like a cricket match, a football match, an open bowls tournament, a treasure hunt etc. While all this is going on there is a fun fair in the market place.

The second procession is held on the first Sunday in August. This is the Civic Procession when Mayor and dignitaries in full regalia process from the Town Hall to the Cathedral in honour of St. Wilfrid.

And while all the celebrations are going on, the Ripon Races take place with the great St. Wilfrid Handicap (the North's richest sprint handicap).

The Ripon Horn Blower still appears at 9pm, while the fun fair is going on in the market place.

Burnsall Feast, Sports and Fell Race

Burnsall is a small village in a remote part of Wharfdale, North Yorkshire.

Some say that the Feast, Sports and Fell Races go back to Elizabethan times, but there is no evidence that this is so. The earliest reference to Burnsall Feast is a report in the *Yorkshire Pioneer* of 1872, which said:

"The Feast passed off very quietly – a marked contrast betwixt those of former Feasts, principally through the new Licensing Act being enforced. After 11pm, the solitary policeman had the Feast entirely to himself."

According to the locals, "It feels that the Sports have been going on well before 1872." Maybe they're right.

The races etc., used to take place on St Wilfrid's day (the church is dedicated to St. Wilfrid) which is 1st August. When in 1752 the calendar was changed by adding 11 days to the year, so the Burnsall people adjusted the date. The activities now take place on the first Saturday following the first Sunday after the 12th August.

The events of the day include a Flower Festival in St Wilfrid's Church, a cycle road race, a ten-mile road walking race, fly casting, a clay pigeon shooting competition, and of course the children have their races to compete in. The main event of the day, however, is the Fell Race, In the past the men taking part in the race turned up in their hobnailed boots and corduroys, but now the runners are well equipped with proper running shoes, shorts etc. The fell is 1,345 feet and the time that it takes is 14 minutes 20 seconds (this is the timing for one year), but the times change every year. The ascent of the fell is the hard part, by having to run up a rugged surface. If a runner is the first to reach the top of the fell, it doesn't mean that he is the winner,

because the descent can take a few minutes to reach the bottom. The women also have a fell race, and their ascent is 1,000 feet. The numbers taking part vary, but there have been up to over 80 taking part.

The fell race is the final race of the day and this starts at 5.30 pm. Then everyone retires to either the pub or the small fun fair, everyone having had a wonderful exciting day, and looking forward to next year's events.

KIRKBY HILL RACES

Such a strange name for an unusual custom. When you see the title of this custom, you immediately think of people having a good run in the hills or the dales. This is not true; it is in fact an election of two wardens to administer almshouses in Kirkby Hill.

It all started in 1556 when the Rector of Kirby Ravensworth, the Rev. Dr. John Dakyn, founded the Almshouses of St. John the Baptist at Kirkby Hill, near Richmond, and he laid down definite rules for the conduct of the place.

Perhaps the most curious of the statutes which were created for the proper administration of the trust, was that dealing with the appointment of wardens to carefully manage and undertake the care and custody of the Almshouses. It provides for an elaborate ceremony by which two of the six of the gravest and most honest men of the parish are impartially selected to fill the office of wardens for two years.

The custom takes place on the day of the Beheading of St. John the Baptist (August 29th).

The tenants of the Almshouses are men and women over retirement age, also those with a disability, and they must have lived in the district for over ten years. The building is now known as the John Dakyn House, and has been renovated over the years and now has six self-contained flats.

Rev. John Dakyn left money in his will so that the men in the almshouses would receive a new suit every two years, likewise the ladies received a new dress. This no longer happens, and the residents do not have to, on oath, abide by the rules of the will, nor do they have to say prayers each day to remember their benefactor. But they are very thankful that they do live in their flats rent and rates-free, and laundry is also paid for.

Every two years, two wardens of the almshouses are voted for. This is a strange ceremony in that there are six men recommended by the Vicar, the Churchwardens, etc., who would be suitable to act as wardens. The names are written down on a slip of paper and then the names are covered with wax (the local cobbler used to do this). The six wax balls are put into a bowl that has been filled with water. The Vicar is then expected to pull out two balls, the Vicar cuts the wax and the name of the person written on the piece of paper is announced to those attending. Likewise the second ball is cut, etc. The two new wardens then have to swear on oath that they will look after the tenants and look after their welfare, etc.

The oldest churchwarden stirring the wax pellets in the pitcher, while the vicar looks on. On the right is the local cobbler who, for nine years, hs encased the names of the nominees in cobbler's wax

The four remaining wax balls are left in the bowl with the water covering them, and it is put away in a cupboard and left there until the next election in two years. The reason for this is that if any one of the two wardens should die, then the bowl is got out again, and another ball is taken out and that person joins the other warden.

All this activity takes place in the school hall, the school having been built by Rev. Dr. John Dakyn.

The custom is known locally as Kirkby Hill Races, and it would be most interesting to learn the origin of that title.

BURNING OWD BARTLE, WEST WILTON

West Wilton is a small village in Wensleydale in North Yorkshire, The custom is not a large affair, but the villagers all join in with great gusto.

"Owd Bartle" is a life size effigy stuffed with straw, and the men who made him parade him through the village with his eyes shining, lit by batteries, which makes the effigy very scary. He is paraded around the village visiting certain places like the pubs, etc., but at each stop the carriers are presented with a drink of whisky and brandy. This, of course, is a luck symbol. Each house, etc., that is visited brings luck to that building and the family within.

At each stop in the village the following verse is shouted:

> At Pen Hill Crag he tore his rag,
> At Hunters Thorn he blew his horn,
> At Capplebank Stee (stile) he brake his knee,
> At Griskill (Grasgill) Beck he brake his neck,
> At Waddams End he couldn't fend,
> At Griskill End will be his end.
> Shout, boys, shout.

According to one local man there is a line missing from this doggerel, which is:

> At Stoney Gate he brake his pate.

At the end of the tour, a knife is plunged into dear old Bartle and he is then set on fire.

So, who is "Bartle"? There are many stories telling us the tale of what is supposed to have happened. Here are some of them.

Bartle was a notorious sheep stealer who lived at Pen Hill in the 17th century, and the local men assembled a posse and killed him at Grassgill End. Another version is that the Pen Hill Giant, who used to steal the sheep from the farmers, was killed by the village men, and was buried on the West Wilton side of Pen Hill. The grave is long enough to hold ten normal men. There is a story is that he was an outlaw who stole swine from the villagers. After a long time the village people decided to round up the outlaw and teach him a lesson. They chased him around the area, and at certain places they caused him many injuries.

Some local people say it is a custom attached to the Harvest. Others think that "Owd Bartle" was a forest god of fertility. Another link is the belief that it is to do with the massacre of the Huguenots on St. Bartholomew's Eve in 1592.

Another version that could possibly be true is that a monk said to be from Jervaulx Abbey used to call on villagers and demand anything he fancied from them to be handed over. It is said that he would enter a house and look around and anything he liked he would demand it. The result eventually brought about hatred from the villagers. The monk is said to have suffered a sad fate.

The church is dedicated to St. Bartholomew, and the custom takes place on the Saturday nearest to St. Bartholomew's Day (24th August). So could it be a very old ceremony attached to St Bartholomew? Who knows?

SEAMER WATERSIDE SERVICE

Seamer Water is two miles south of Askrigg. The lake in the summer months is a hive of activity in that there are crowds of people water-skiing, motor boats racing around, with plenty of sunbathers and picnics. Lots of laughter, shouting and general chat, but on the last Sunday in August all is quiet, because there in a boat is the local vicar generally overseeing a religious service.

The idea of a lakeside service was brought about by the then Vicar of Askrigg. Having passed Seamer Water many times, he thought that it would be an ideal situation to hold a service. So this he did on the last Sunday in August.

The service was a great success, and the local church council organised for the next year's service, a bus to get the congregation to the lakeside.

The music supplied initially was played by a local accordionist, and as the congregation increased a harmonium was brought in to play, and again the crowd got larger so the Hawes Silver Band were asked to play for the service.

The Vicar of Askrigg and Stelling Busk is carried pick-a-back to the boat, where he then conducts a short service with a sermon preached from the boat. He is then carried back to the lakeside.

LEE GAP HORSE FAIR

Stallions proud and ribbands prancing
Joyous fiddling and dancing

Isaac Horsfield who was there
He made sport for all the fair.

A handsome show of china ware
Of much variety was there

Cheesecakes plenty might be got
Gingerbread and good tom-trot.

The fair was founded over 800 years ago, not long after the church, which is dedicated to St. Mary. The fair took place on the Feast of the Assumption (8th September) and finished on the Nativity of the Blessed Virgin (15th August). King Stephen confirmed this charter, and

some time afterwards the fair began to be held nine days later. Until the end of the 18th century it was, in fact, a single fair lasting from 24th August (St. Bartholomew's) until 17th September. Nowadays the fairs are held only on the first date and the last one.

People travelled vast distances to be part of the Lee Gap Fair. Many took the opportunity of getting married or having their children baptised, often at the same time.

The fair takes place on two days, one on 24th August and the other on

17th September, known as the former and the latter. Over the years there has been a certain amount of drunkenness, bloodshed, damage to property, etc. The residents had to suffer this unpleasantness twice a year, and in 1656 the inhabitants petitioned the justices of the West Riding requesting that the fair be abolished as it was a nuisance, and the Wakefield Market met their needs.

Woodkirk Fair: detail from a stained glass window in the church

At the dissolution of the monasteries, Nostell Priory was granted to a Dr. Leigh, and the canons held the fair at their church at Woodkirk, otherwise known as West Ardsley, which became known as Lee Gap Fair.

In the Middle Ages Lee Gap Fair attracted merchants from France, Spain, Florence and the low lands of Germany, plus families of consequence as well as the religious houses in this country. Horses, cattle, sheep, goats and other livestock were sold at the fair. It seems that Lee Gap Fair was the place to be seen.

Alas, it is no longer such a spectacular fair, but it is still going with a few horses being sold by the shaking of the hand. Like most fairs in England, there is an amusement park with roundabouts, large swings and stalls.

SEPTEMBER

SEPTENNIAL BOUUNDARY RIDE, RICHMOND

Numa Pompilius, the second of Rome's early kings, is thought to be the first person to institute the practice of boundary perambulations as homage to Terminus, the god of boundaries and landmarks.

The Riding of the Bounds at Richmond started for the first time after 1576, in the time of Elizabeth I.

The Riding of the Bounds is performed every seven years. The next will take place in 2011 (2018, 2025).

This is very much a civic affair, with all the local aldermen and councillors going in procession visiting the Boundaries. At a date in September every seven years all those in the procession assemble at the Town Hall, and at 8.30am or around that time, the procession moves out. The procession is very impressive and very colourful, with:

The Banner Bearers (carrying the old banner of the Richmond Coat of
   Arms)
Two Halbardiers
Two Mace Bearers (carrying both large and small maces)
Two Sergeants at Mace
The Mayor (carrying his mace)
The Town Clerk
The Pinder (who carries an axe to clear away any obstruction)
The Bellman
The Town Crier
The Water Wader (who carries the Mayor into the middle of the
   River Swale, which is a boundary mark)
The Alderman

The Councillors
The Burgesses

At certain places on the journey, the Town Crier declares:

"Oyez, Oyez, Oyez

I do in the name of the Mayor, Aldermen and Burgesses of the Boroughs of Richmond, Lords of the Manor and Borough of Richmond in the County of Yorkshire, hereby proclaim and declare this to be the ancient and undoubted

Carrying the Mayor across the river Swale

boundary of the said Manor and Borough against the Manor or Lordship of......................... God save the Queen and the Lords of the Manor."

Likewise at certain places on the journey pennies are thrown at the crowd. There are also stops made for refreshments.

The Boundaries are around 16 miles in all, and there is now provision for those who have taken part and completed the walk to receive a certificate signed by the Mayor to say that "they had done it".

Hundreds of people take part in this very happy and jovial custom. Long may it live.

**TOWN OF RICHMOND
BOUNDARY RIDING**

I give notice that pursuant to the charters of Queen Elizabeth I (1576) and King Charles II (1666) and following custom faithfully observe since those times the boundary of the Borough of Richmond in the County of York will be ridden and perambulated by the Council of the said Borough, the Lords of the Manor of Richmond aforesaid, its Agents and others on

WEDNESDAY 25 AUGUST 2004

Dr Peter Clark
Town Clerk

This is to certify that

*completed the 2004 Septennial
Boundary Riding*

Town May

Town Cle

Master Cutler Election, Sheffield

The Company of Cutlers in Hallamshire was founded in 1624 to oversee the cutlery trades (knives, scissors, shears, razors, etc.) in Hallamshire, a small Anglo-Saxon division of the country centred on Sheffield. From that date until 1814 ALL cutlery apprentices had to have their indentures enrolled at the Cutlers' Hall. Only Freemen of the Company were allowed a trademark, and no-one was allowed to sell cutlery that was not stamped with a trademark. To become a Freeman you had to have served a minimum of seven years apprenticeship under an existing Freeman and be at least 21 years old. But in the early years of the 19th century, things changed dramatically. An Act of Parliament passed in 1814 removed the legal obligation to register apprenticeships, and cutlery factories began to be built employing hundreds of men, either directly or as outworkers, who did not need their own trademark because they were making cutlery that was being stamped with a Company mark. According to the 1881 Census, there were 18,000 cutlers working in England, 15,000 of them in Sheffield.

Since 1860 Freemen have had to work for companies that manufacture cutlery and tools of steel within the area and membership has been voluntary, but there are currently just over 400 Freemen.

Every year 33 Freemen are chosen to govern the Cutlers' Company, and they are known collectively as "The Company" and individually as "Members". They are headed by the Master Cutler, followed by the Senior Warden, Junior Warden, six Searchers and twenty-four Assistants. Originally the Company was chosen on August 25th, the Feast Day of St Bartholomew, the patron saint of Cutlers, but now they are chosen on the first Monday in September and are installed on the first Tuesday in October.

The highlight of the Master Cutlers' year is the Cutlers' Feast, a dinner which has been held almost every year since 1625. It is a very formal occasion (white tie, etc.) and guests include Members of Parliament, foreign diplomats, heads of armed forces, captains of industry and local civic dignitaries. Principal guests have included seven serving Prime Ministers, eight Chancellors of the Exchequer, three Lord Chancellors and six Archbishops.

INSTALLATION

OF THE

MASTER CUTLER

THE CUTLERS' HALL, SHEFFIELD

OCTOBER

AGENDA

1. The Master Cutler-elect to make and subscribe the Oath and make the Declaration.
2. The Master Cutler-elect to be invested by the retiring Master Cutler with the badge of office.
3. The Wardens to make and subscribe the Oath, make the Declaration and be invested by the Master Cutler with their Badges of Office.
4. The Searchers to qualify.

Declaration of a Searcher

I.   DO solemnly, sincerely and truly DECLARE and AFFIRM that 1 will to the best of my ability, justly, indifferently and impartially keep, do and execute, and cause to be kepi, done and executed all and every the good, lawful and laudable Acts. Laws and Ordinances made for the regulation and government of the Company of Cutlers in Hallamshire in the County of'York without sparing or impeaching any person or persons whomsoever for affection or malice or for or in respect of any reward or promise of reward during the time that I may hold the office of a Searcher.AND of all goods, chattels and sums of money as by reason of my said Office may come to my hands I will within a reasonable time deliver over into the hands and custody of the Master and Wardens for the time being of the said Company Or some one of them and make a true, due, just and plain account thereof.

SO HELP ME GOD.

5. The Assistants to qualify.

Declaration of an Assistant

1,   DO solemnly, sincerely and truly DECLARE and AFFIRM that I will to the best of my ability so far as I lawfully may give and use my faithful advice and counsel to the Master and Wardens of the Company of Cutlers in Hallamshire in the County of York for the time being for the better execution of their said offices AND shall give and use my faithful aid and assistance in every respect as much as in me lieth and lawfully I may do for the due observance of all the good lawful and laudable Acts, Laws and Ordinances of the said Company according to the true intent and meaning of the same without sparing or impeaching any person or persons whomsoever for affection or malice or for or in respect of any reward or promise of reward during the time that I shall hold the office of an ASSISTANT.

SO HELP ME GOD.

6. The newly installed Master to address the Company.

7. The Master to propose " That the best thanks of the Company be given to Mr. and Mrs. Hugh Sykes for their services as Master and Mistress Cutler during the past year".

Mr. John McGee to second the proposal.

8. The Past Master,   , to reply.

9. The Clerk to speak.

10. **MOTION AS TO FINES ON NON-ATTENDANCE**

That each member of the Company neglecting to attend any General Meeting called by the Master Cutler or his representative, after receiving due notice of the same shall forfeit for every such neglect 5p on his neglecting to answer his name on the first call, and 10p on the second call; and it is ordered that at each meeting so convened the names of the Members shall be called over twice, and that the Master Cutler, or other person presiding shall direct the times for calling over the names.

11. TO APPOINT THE FOLLOWING as MEMBERS OF THE FINANCE
COMMITTEE:-

12. TO APPOINT THE FOLLOWING as MEMBERS OF THE HALLS
COMMITTEE:-

13. TO APPOINT THE FOLLOWING as MEMBERS OF THE LOCAL AFFAIRS
COMMITTEE:-

14. TO APPOINT THE FOLLOWING as MEMBERS OF THE EDUCATION
COMMITTEE:-

(Chairman)

The Master Cutler

The Senior Warden

The Junior Warden

15. TO APPOINT THE FOLLOWING as MEMBERS OF THE MASTER'S
ADVISORY COMMITTEE:

The Senior Warden   The Junior Warden   The Immediate Past Master

Senior Searcher

Chairman: Finance Committee

Chairman: Halls Committee

Chairman: Local Affairs Committee

Chairman: Education Committee

Chairman: Preservation Trust Council of Management

16. TO APPOINT as SHEFFIELD DEFENCE ADVISOR: -

17. 10 APPOINT as FREEDOMS ADVISOR:*

18. TO CONFIRM THE FOLLOWING as MEMBERS OF THE SEARCHERS
COMMITTEE:

The Master Cutler   The Senior Warden   The Junior Warden and the Searchers for the time being.

19. MOTION AS TO MEETINGS OF THE COMPANY:-

That Meetings of the Company be held as the Master Cutler may deem to be necessary.

ORDER OF PROCESSIONS

TO THE OLD BANQUETING HALL
The Deputy Beadle
The Mistress Cutlers Procession
The Lord Lieutenant
The High Sheriff   ) and
The Lord Mayor of Sheffield) their
The Mayor of Rotherham   ) Ladies/
The Mayor of Barnsley   ) Consort
The Clerk
The Past Masters by seniority
The Chaplain
The Wardens Elect
The Beadle
The Master Cutler, The Master Cutler
        elect

FROM THE OLD BANQUETING
HALL
The Beadle
The Master Cutler, the Immediate Past
        Master
The Wardens
The Chaplain
The Past Masters by seniority
The Searchers
The Assistants
The Clerk
The Lord Lieutenant
The High Sheriff   ) and
The Lord Mayor of Sheffield) their
The Mayor of Rotherham   ) Ladies/
The Mayor of Barnsley   ) Consort
The Deputy Beadle
The Mistresses Cutlers Procession
The Masters Family
Personal Guests
The Freemen

FROM THE CUTLERS' HALL TO
THE CATHEDRAL
Freemen, Family and Guests
The Deputy Beadle
The Mistress Cutlers Procession
The Lord Lieutenant
The High Sheriff   ) and
The Lord Mayor of Sheffield) their
The Mayor of Rotherham   ) Ladies/
The Mayor of Barnsley   ) Consort
The Clerk
The Beadle
The Master Cutler, the Immediate Past
        Master
The Wardens
The Past Masters by reverse seniority
The Searchers
The Assistants

FROM THE CATHEDRAL TO THE
CUTLERS' HALL
The Dean
The Lord Lieutenant
The High Sheriff   ) and
The Lord Mayor of Sheffield) their
The Mayor of Rotherham   ) Ladies/
The Mayor of Barnsley   ) Consort
The Beadle
The Master Cutler, the Immediate Past
        Master
The Wardens
The Clerk
The Past Masters by seniority
The Searchers
The Assistants
The Deputy Beadle
The Mistress Cutlers Procession
The Masters Family
Personal Guests
The Freemen

Oath of Master

I,_____

do swear that I will be faithful and bear true

allegiance to Her Majesty Queen Elizabeth II her

heirs and successors according to law.

So help me God

Taken and Subscribed
at Sheffield this
day of October   *Master Cutler*

Senior Warden

Junior Warden

DECLARATION OF A MASTER/WARDEN

I, ...

DO SOLEMNLY, SINCERELY AND TRULY DECLARE AND AFFIRM THAT I WILL TO THE BEST OF MY ABILITY, JUSTLY, INDIFFERENTLY AND IMPARTIALLY KEEP, DO AND EXECUTE AND CAUSE TO BE KEPT DONE AND EXECUTED, ALL AND EVERY THE GOOD, LAWFUL AND LAUDABLE ACTS, LAWS AND ORDINANCES MADE FOR THE REGULATION AND GOVERNMENT OF THE COMPANY OF CUTLERS' IN HALLAMSHIRE IN THE COUNTY OF YORK, WITHOUT SPARING OR IMPEACHING ANY PERSON OR PERSONS WHOMSOEVER, FROM AFFECTION OR MALICE OR FOR IN RESPECT OF ANY REWARD OR PROMISE OF REWARD DURING THE TIME I SHALL HOLD THE OFFICE OF *JUNIOR WARDEN* AND OF ALL SUCH GOODS, CHATTELS AND SUMS OF MONEY AS BY REASON OF MY SAID OFFICE SHALL COME TO MY HANDS, I, ACCORDING TO THE ACTS, LAWS AND ORDINANCES ABOVE SPECIFIED SHALL MAKE A TRUE, DUE, JUST AND PLAIN ACCOUNT, AND I WILL NOT FOR MALICE NOR FOR LOVE OR AFFECTION AMERCE ANY PERSON IN A GREATER OR LESS SUM THAN AFTER THE QUANTITY OR QUALITY OF HIS OFFENCE ACCORDING TO THE SAID ACTS, LAWS AND ORDINANCES.

SO HELP ME GOD

RUSH CART, SOWERBY BRIDGE

Not so long ago practically all churches, particularly the country churches, set aside a special day when the whole village brought rushes, either in procession or individually, to church to lay on the stone floor. This was the time when there was no form of heating, and the rushes kept the church dry and warm. Some villages made a special effort by getting the congregation to process through the village to the church, and then the rushes were spread over the floor.

Sowerby Bridge, however, made the ceremony very important by dressing the "Rushcart", a two or four-wheel cart that has a special shape, built with rushes, with a man astride the top. The rushcart in years gone by could be seen in areas around Huddersfield and Halifax.

Sowerby Bridge Rushcart disappeared in the 1840's. It was revived in 1906 to celebrate 60 years of local government. As part of the event, a grand procession was organised, with floats displaying activities that had disappeared over the past 60 years, and of course the rushcart was part of the celebrations. It looks as though this revival was just for the year 1906.

The recent revival took place in 1977, and is still going strong. The rushcart is pulled by the Sowerby Bridge Morris Men. The procession proceeds along a set route visiting different areas around Sowerby Bridge. Their first stop is in Warley at the site of the Maypole and outside the inn of the same name. There are also dance displays at certain stops.

The celebration takes place on the first weekend in September.

MASHAM SHEEP FAIR

The original fair was granted by Charter in 1250 to John de Wauton, to take place on the Feast of the Assumption in September. In 1393 a Stephen le Scrope became the new owner, and he changed the date of the fair to the Feast of the Assumption of the Blessed Virgin Mary, the patron saint of the church at Masham. The fair took place from the 16th to 18th September. Now the fair is held on 6th - 8th September.

Masham Sheep Fair – 1905

Stephen le Scrope was also granted a charter to hold a second fair on St. Barnabas Day (11th June).

The fair is situated in the market place. The visitor to Masham nearly always comments on the market place as being uncommonly spacious.

The farmers brought their butter, eggs and cheese to sell at the market, and they bought and sold their cattle and sheep. Also it is where they bought all the cloth to make clothing for the family for the next twelve months until the fair next year. The pens to house the sheep were erected in the market place, but over-spilled along the road from the market place, which meant the pens were erected outside the residents' houses, much to the joy of the children.

The Cistercians from France settled in the Yorkshire Dales. The Abbots of Fountains and Jervaulx by the 13th Century became the largest sheep-keepers in Europe.

The Masham fair was a very successful event, and attracted thousands of sheep and thousands of visitors, until the First World War and the Depression afterwards forced the fair to close down. A revival in 1986 has brought the Masham Sheep Fair back as it was before it stopped, and it is now attracting many different breeds to the market-place and streets of Masham. Other attractions are a flower festival and craft festival, morris dancing, a children's fair and performances from local brass bands.

The breeding of sheep in the area started with two horned hill breeds, the Swaledale and the Dales breed and the Blue-faced Leicester crossed with a Teeswater or a Wensleydale to produce a Masham.

First Fruits, Richmond

Although no-one seems to know the age of this custom, it has been suggested by one local historian that it goes back to medieval times. The people were very dependent on the success of each year's harvest. Corn was grown on the three great open fields north of the town, known as Westfield, Gallowfield and Eastfield.

The origin of the First Fruits Ceremony goes back to when the Castle at Richmond was occupied. Perhaps the tradition started when some official, fearing a siege from the marauding Scots, encouraged the local husbandmen to bring their grain to the Castle for safe keeping as soon as the produce was harvested, and rewarding in some way the first to do so. Today the First Fruits ceremony still takes place

on a Saturday in September and a token reward (a bottle of wine) is presented by the Mayor of Richmond on receiving a "goodly sample" of wheat.

The presentation ceremony is preceded by a short service of thanksgiving for the harvest in Holy Trinity Church in the Market Square. Before the actual presentation the Mayor will call upon a corn merchant to verify that the sample is in fact wheat and is in good condition. After that the Mayor presents a bottle of wine to the farmer with the first fruits.

It is customary for the farmer to open the bottle of wine and invite the assembled company to join him in a drink. This seems very mean when the farmer who worked hard at his wheat growing is expected to share his bottle of wine with all those in attendance, but the farmer is in fact given two bottles of wine, one to be opened to drink in Market Square and one to be drunk at home.

But many, many years ago a barrel of beer was presented in the Market Square, and that was offered to the Mayor and public – a much better idea.

Yarm (Cheese) Fair

Yarm is on the River Tees and surrounded by the river in a horseshoe shape. Just over a bridge, and you're in North Yorkshire.

It is believed that King John granted a charter to hold a three-day fair in Yarm. It is true that King John, when granting Liberty of Langbaugh to Peter de Brus, Lord of Skelton, in 1207, gave him the right to hold a weekly market every Thursday and to hold two annual one-day fairs on the feast of the Ascension and that of St. Mary Magdalene, the town's patron saint, whose Festival is on the 22nd July. This charter was granted to Peter de Brus and not to the town of Yarm, and it does refer to a fair in October.

When Thomas Bellasis of Newburgh Priory, the first Baron Fanconburgh of Yarm, disposed of the Liberty of Langbaugh in 1631, the market and fair rights went with it, presumably to the regret of the Bellasis family, who were Lords of the Manor of Yarm. Thomas, grandson of the above, tried in vain to recover them, but was unsuccessful. However, King Charles II in 1674 granted a new fair. So the October fair was born.

Back in the mid 1800's the fair was a thriving affair when it was held on the 19th and 20th October, with the 19th being for horned cattle and horses and the 20th being for sheep and cheese. When the third day was added, this was devoted to cattle, sheep and cheese. It was regarded as the biggest Fair of the North-East of England for cheese. To give you an idea, for a few years 500 tons of cheese was carried into Yarm with over 400 horse-drawn carts stacked high with cheese, and the amazing thing was all the cheese was sold at the fair. The cheese was sold on the road unprotected; imagine the fears of the modern-day Trading Standards witnessing such a happening! The fair attracted many people, traders and gypsies from all over the country, and it wasn't uncommon for 3,500 horses to be shipped over from Ireland. The Gypsies say that is their fair, and they would set up stalls, booths etc. for fortune-telling by cards or crystal ball. The fair was, and still is, held in the High Street.

The fair has to be officially opened by the reading of the proclamation, but before that a four-foot horn is blown to attract the crowd. The proclamation is then read thus:

The parish council for the town of Yarm in the County of Yorkshire give Notice that their fair in, and for the said, town will be holden by them as charter authorised, this day and tomorrow for the sale of cattle, goods and merchandise or whatsoever, that the same shall be and endure until tomorrow evening at six of the clock and no longer, when all persons selling merchandise shall close their stalls and booths under pain of forfeiting double the value of the goods, and all persons buying merchandise in the said fair and not immediately paying the usual tolls for the same to the Parish Council, or to whom they may appoint to receive the same, will be prosecuted as the law directs. Dated this day 19th October (year). God Save the Queen.

Sadly, the fair today is just a funfair, with roundabouts, coconut shies etc., with the Gypsies doing what they have done at Yarm Fair for centuries.

OCTOBER

KINGSTON UPON HULL HORSE FAIR

The first charter for a market and a fair was applied for by the Abbot of Meux in 1278. This was granted in 1279 as follows: "Grant to the Abbey and Convent of Meux of a weekly market on Thursday at their manor of Wyke super le Hull, County of York, and of a yearly fair there on the vigil, the feast and the morrow of Holy Trinity and the twelve days following."

The town of Kingston upon Hull was then founded when King Edward I acquired Wyke upon Hull on the 31st January, 1293. Whilst spending Christmas at Barnard Castle he was presented with a petition by the inhabitants of Kingston upon Hull for many privileges, which included a market on Tuesday and Friday and a 30-day fair. This was granted.

Over the years there have been a few new charters granted, all of which were asking for markets on Tuesday and Friday plus a horse fair running for 30 days.

The horse fair was a very popular event attracting hundreds of people every year. The selling of horses, cattle, sheep, lambs etc. were all part of this function, plus of course the stalls manned by pedlars, shoemakers, linen drapers and sellers of wooden ware and hardware.

Because of an Act of Parliament in 1752 correcting the calendar to the one used today, the Hull Quarter Sessions held on 27th August 1752 suggested that the horse fair be held on the 10th October and not on the 29th September. This new date has been kept ever since.

The horse fair continued selling cattle etc, but as the years went by, it was apparent that the fair was becoming a pleasure fair and not a horse fair. So it got to the stage that it is in today, a very, very large funfair.

FISHERMENS' HARVEST FESTIVAL

Flamborough is a small village on the north-east coast of the East Riding of Yorkshire, a fishermen's village, although in recent years the fishing trade has reduced considerably. The people of Flamborough are very proud of their lifeboat, which is of course on call twenty-four hours a day.

Not so long ago there was a special service held in St. Oswald's Parish Church, St. Oswald being the patron saint of fishermen. This was the Fishermen's Harvest Festival on the second Sunday in October. The church was decorated with crab pots and fishing nets.

As stated before, the fishing at Flamborough has declined. And of the forty or more cobles that went fishing from Flamborough Head, only about four are left.

The Fishermen's Harvest Service was a full church service with hymns, prayers, etc., and the Blessing of the Fishermen was done within this ceremony.

The service nowadays is a part of evening prayers, with two appropriate readings, one from the Old Testament and one from the New, the second being read by one of the current lifeboat crew. The hymns that are sung are suitably nautical, i.e. Eternal Father, Jesu Lover of my Soul, and Pull for the Shore Sailor.

Seeing that the lifeboat and its crew are so important to the people of Flamborough and surrounding areas, a special service is held in July in and around the Lifeboat Station. This service is known as "The Lifeboat Songs of Praise" and in part of the service the lifeboat and crew are blessed by the Vicar of Flamborough.

COURT LEET

The old Manorial Courts (Courts Leet) met regularly to regulate such matters as rents and tenures, the state of roads and houses, and other questions affecting the lives of people who live in the districts covered by their jurisdictions.

Many local matters are thus amicably settled which might otherwise lead to disputes between landlord and tenant, and it would be a great loss to more than antiquarians if these ancient courts were finally abolished.

In 1977 the Government decided to "rationalise" the local court systems, and it abolished all local courts but a select few thought to be efficiently serving their local communities. Danby was clearly one of the few survivors, there being only twelve Courts Leet left in the country.

Danby. Greeholders are summoned to be admitted to their rights on the common – the fine of 5p is collected in the bowl in front of the baliff who sits next to Lord Downe's steward

Danby is a few miles west of Whitby and as stated above still performing the annual Court Leet. The Court is held each year in Danby Castle, once the home of Catherine Parr, which has been owned by the Dawney family since the mid-seventeenth century. The Court can be traced back to the fourteenth century.

Records show that it was fining the citizens of Danby for brewing

Danby Castle

without a licence, trespassing with "unringed" pigs and keeping too many sheep. It is interesting to note that some of the procedures of the Court, such as swearing allegiance and kissing the Bible, go back to before the Reformation.

Commoners have an obligation to attend the annual Court and are fined "tuppence" which hasn't changed since the Reformation.

The Court usually meet in October each year.

The present day Court is run by the Bailiff and a Jury with a Foreman. The reason that it runs so smoothly is because those on the Jury have a detailed knowledge of the extent of Danby Common and the rights over it.

The importance of the Court is nicely summarised by a poem read out by the Jury Foreman that is on page 88.

The day is finished with an excellent and lavish dinner.

Court Leet:
Downe v Thompson

Based on the Whitby Times of 1
December 1893 at Pannet Park
Museum.

A Publican of Castleton,
in eighteen ninety three,
said "Danby's silly notions
have nowt to do with me".

So he ignored the Court Leet,
when summoned to attend.
Although, no doubt, he wished that
he had gone there in the end.

He could have paid them tuppence
just like other absentees:

The Court Leet had no wishes
to bring him to his knees.

So they fined the man three shillings,
which may not seem a lot,
but back in those Victorian days
it's more than some had got.

When taken to the County Court,
because he didn't pay,
the Judge and all the lawyers there
had quite a pleasant day.

Joe Thompson, the publican,
said he had no Common Rights
and very little money
and lots of sleepless nights.

As a freeborn Englishman
he knew that justice would prevail,
so he'd accept the verdict
whatever that entail.

He named some other tenants,
who hadn't paid at all,
so clearly it was wrong
that he should suffer from them all.

The judge replied if he chose
to put Thompson in the nick,
he thought the other tenants
would pay up pretty quick!

He explained the law existed
to protect the common good
whilst absent Irish landlords
did everything they could.

Obstinate, unruly people
must be taught to see
the advantages of living
in a country that is free.

He said that Thompson's case
was based on very shaky ground
so he'd have to pay the penalty
of something near ten pound

There's a moral to this story,
though it isn't very clear,
but you get more money at the Bar
than selling bottled beer!

B C Mayston

89

COURT LEET Almondbury

Almondbury is now a district of Huddersfield in the West Riding of Yorkshire.

The Court Leet still meets twice a year, one within the month next after Michaelmas, the other within the month next after Easter.

The Court involves members from Huddersfield, Hanley, Meltham, South Grosland, Skerthwaite and Quick (Saddleworth). The Court with its Jury are there to hear the "cases of affray, bloods and other common annoyances" which had been committed within all the townships.

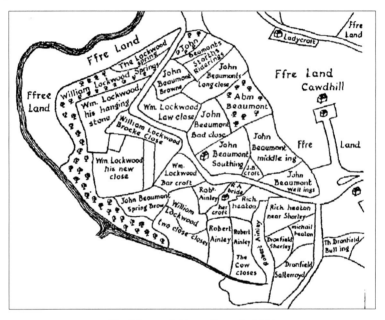

The Manor of Almondbury in 1634
This map first appeared in Taylor Dyson's 'History of Huddersfield',
drawn by N.L. Houslop: redrawn by A. Boughey

COURT LEET, Mickley

Mickley is a small village with one main street, no street lights, no shops and no pubs and is about six miles from Ripon.

The Court Leet at Mickley is no different to the others, except that it meets every three years. The jury is made up of residents who rent their premises and do not own them, The jury, after being sworn, views the different properties of the Manor and draws up a report in the form of a verdict on the state of the properties and advises what repairs should be done. This verdict is presented to the Lords for their consideration and decision. The proceedings are always accompanied by a dinner paid for out of the accumulated rents of the property, at which the Loyal Toast and that of the Manor of Mickley are drunk.

The proceedings take place in a pub near to the village.

NOVEMBER

CAKING NIGHT, DUNGWORTH AND STANNINGTON

The Celtic Festival of Sambain is on 1st November, and the Celts believed that on this day all the souls of the dead were abroad. At this time, when the boundaries between light and dark, life and death, new and old were thin, the dead returned to their old haunts, and it was easier for spirits to walk abroad disguised as men.

Dungworth and Stannington, just outside Sheffield, keep the memory of this Celtic Custom, known as Caking Night or Kakin Night. Before the Second World War it was performed by children getting dressed up in a variety of costumes, the idea being to visit all the houses in the village. At each house the people answering the door

were expected to recognise the children, and if they were incorrect, money would be given to the children. If on the other hand they were identified, tharf (?) cakes would be given. These cakes were made from oatmeal, butter and treacle. Although the children are in fancy dress, they also disguise their voices when they knock on the door, and shout "Copper Copper Cake Cake."

Since the war the custom has changed in that those taking part today are adults as well as children, all of whom dress up. The adults' fancy dress is usually as witches, ghosts, ghouls, etc., all in keeping with the Festival of Sambain when the souls

92

returned to earth.

The evening starts around 5.30pm, and just before the pub opens the children go to an upstairs room to have their costumes judged. When the pub opens it is the turn of the adults to have their costumes judged. First prize was one pound, second 75p, third 50p. The prizes hopefully increased over the years.

It is certain that what takes place today is very much a watered down version of what used to happen, but it is a good example of the Christian Church taking a Pagan Custom under their wing, and it is now November 1st, All Souls Eve, and November 2nd, All Souls Day.

DECEMBER

CAROL SINGING IN SOUTH YORKSHIRE

A small area in South Yorkshire is the home of a very unique tradition that takes place from November to Christmas. That is the Pub Carol Singing tradition just north and west of Sheffield.

The Royal Hotel, Dungworth

According to a local man, the carols that are sung in the pub were rejected by the Victorian chapel-goers because they were too happy and jolly. Surely this is what carols should be, seeing that it is such a happy time.

There are a few well-known carols like *While Shepherds Watched Their Flocks by Night*, but most of them are local carols composed by local people.

The pattern of discouraging the singing of these popular songs in churches and chapels seemed to come to a head in the 1920's and 1930's. The reaction of the carollers was simply to take the carols out on to the street corners. This, of course was a very common way to hear the songs being sung in those days.

They would also sing their carols in the big houses in the affluent areas of Sheffield. They would have trombone, fiddle and double bass accompanying them. This singing continued until after the Second World War, and definitely by the 1950's - 1960's the carollers found it a bit hard going in November and December with the weather being what it was at that time of the year. So it was found that if the chapel wouldn't have them the pub was the next best thing. So the tradition continues, but indoors and not outside in the bad weather. There is evidence, however, that pub singing goes back to the 1850's.

The singing in all the pubs is passionate, sincere and enjoyed by everyone. Each pub has its own carols, and the well known carols like *While Shepherds Watched their Flocks by Night* have their own local names. To see someone singing their heart out with a pint of ale in their hands seems to be most natural.

The villages where the pub is a singing pub are:

Bolsterstone	Lodge Moor
Deepcar	Crosspool
Stockbridge	Ringinglow
Wortley	Ladybower
Green Moor	Rivelin
Midhopestone	Stannington
Langsett	Loxley
Thurgoland	Dungworth
Crane Moor	Wadsley
Oxspring	Middlewood
Penistone	Worrall
Thurlstone	Oughtibridge
Millhouse	Wharncliffeside
Ingbirchworth	Bradfield
Strines	

This is just a list of a few places where the carolling takes place. There are other places that are not mentioned. The timing of the singing is from mid-November to the Saturday after Christmas, lunchtime and evening.

It is absolutely incredible that in such a small area, so many places keep this wonderful tradition alive.

AUDIT MONEY, RICHMOND

Richmond in North Yorkshire is a large market town, and is proud of a number of customs that still take place through the year.

The Mayor's Audit Money dates back to Queen Elizabeth I and was first mentioned under that title in the charter of the Queen given to the town in 1576. The town of Richmond under previous charters paid to the Crown a sum of money in respect of the Fee Farm Rent (the Crown land upon which the town of Richmond stood). The Queen decreed that the sum should be returned by her commissioners to the Mayor of the day to be distributed by him to the "poor indigenous tradesmen and decayed house keepers", the distribution to be made just before Christmas.

The Queen's declaration has been continued by the Mayors of Richmond every year since 1576. Over the years there have been a number of changes, and no longer is the dole paid to the poor, but any woman over sixty and any gentleman over sixty-five, as residents of Richmond, qualify for receiving the Audit Money.

Up until 1968 the Mayor used to distribute a coin of the realm (50p), but in that year it was decided by the Mayor and Council that no longer will the Mayor distribute the 50p, but that a special coin should be minted for the occasion. The then Town Clerk was instructed to design a suitable coin and to have the coin struck at the Birmingham Mint. The newly-designed coin was struck in September 1968 and distributed to the residents in December 1968.

The size of the coin was similar to the old florin, and it was named by the people as the Richmond Shilling. The face side is a view of the Richmond Castle on the River Swale. This was based on an old wood-cut of 1700, and has the wording "Mayors Audit Money Richmond North Yorkshire". The reverse side depicts the Richmond Coat of

96

Arms with the words "Mater Omnium Richmundiarum" (the Mother of all Richmonds). There are about fifty-seven other Richmonds throughout the world, and all acknowledge the North Yorkshire Richmond was the original. Also on this side of the coin are the words "Elizabeth Regina 1576".

When the ladies and gentlemen collect the Richmond Shilling from the Mayor in his parlour in the Town Hall, their names are recorded in the ledger of the Audit Money. These records go back to the 1600's. Refreshments are served and a pleasant little social occasion occurs.

In the year 2000 a special, special coin was minted to celebrate the Millennium, and on this occasion not only the pensioners received the new Richmond Shilling but all the school children received the coin as well.

HANGING THE WHEATSHEAF, HIGH ACKWORTH

High Ackworth is situated to the east of Wakefield. The church at Ackworth is dedicated to St. Cuthbert, and over the archway into the church porch is an effigy of St. Cuthbert in full regalia, wearing a cope and mitre and holding a pastoral staff.

On Christmas Eve the local Rector hangs a wheatsheaf on the saint's staff.

The local residents maintain that the custom dates back to the time when West Yorkshire was extensively penetrated by the Vikings. The sheaf was raised by them for the Ravens, who were the mythical messengers for the God Odin.

Although there is no evidence to show how old this custom is, it could be that the sheaf was displayed for the whole community to see that the harvest had been completed. Over the years it went from harvest time to Christmas.

There is a story that an American newspaper reported on the custom by saying that this was an old "horse" (Norse) custom, and that the "Horsemen" hung a sheaf for the Odin Ravens.

Although this is a simple little Custom, it still is an important event for the people of High Ackworth, and of course it is still being performed.

Sword Dance

When a sword dance is mentioned, the thought of two swords lying crossed on the floor with a kilted dancer dancing over the swords comes to mind. That, of course, is the Scottish version of the dance. The English Sword Dance, however, is very different. There are six or eight men in a team, and they dance under the swords creating complicated figures by weaving in and out.

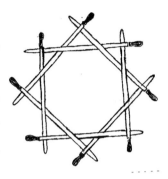

The eight sword lock

Yorkshire is the home of the traditional long sword dance, except for one in Durham. The sword is a strip of metal with a hard handle at one end. Each dancer holds his sword in the right hand and the dancer next to him has to hold the tip of his neighbour's sword, creating a large circle. They then perform the dance by creating complicated figures, finishing with the "lock".

As mentioned before, the traditional long sword is found only in Yorkshire (except for one in County Durham). The Tradition is found in the north-east of Yorkshire around the Whitby area (only one left). Another is just a few miles north-east of Bridlington, and there are two in the Sheffield area.

There is another form of sword dance that can be found in County Durham and Northumberland. Whereas the long sword is usually of rigid metal with a handle at one end, the other dance has a sword that has a handle at each end, and very flexible metal. This is because there are only five dancers and the figures are danced very close together, so a flexible sword is essential.

The long sword dance is quite old, in fact some have said that the dance was performed in pre-Christian times. It would be nice to think that this was true, but there is no evidence to back this theory up.

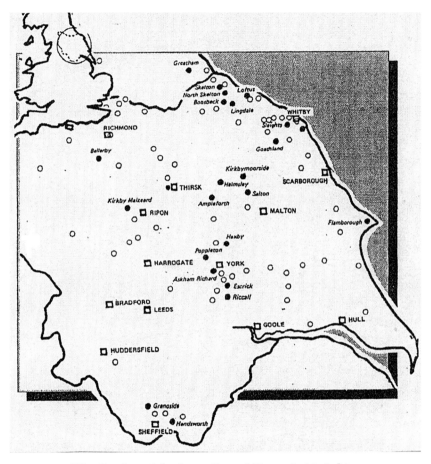

Distribution of the Long Sword Dance in Yorkshire
O Locations which at one time had a long sword dance
● Locations which have a dance recorded in sufficient detail to perform

THE FLAMBOROUGH SWORD DANCE

This dance is a fishermen's dance and the costumes worn are fishermen's "ganseys" (jumpers), white trousers and flat caps. Records of this dance go back more than 150 years. The team consists of eight dancers, carrying the wooden swords in their left hand (all the other teams hold their swords in the right hand). The dance is taught in the village school, so the dancers are always Flamborough people. It also means that a team can be made up at any time. The step used is the skip step, which is unusual because other traditional sword dance teams use a rhythmic walking step.

The date each year that Flamborough Sword Dance is danced around the village is Boxing Day.

HANDSWORTH SWORD DANCE

It is unknown how old the Handsworth dance is. At one time the dance was known as the Handsworth and Woodhouse Traditional Long Sword Dance. The dance shifted to Handsworth village in 1890.

The present team was revived in 1963 after a 46-year lapse. The uniform that the men wear is a black velvet jacket with maroon waistband and cuffs, brass buttons and seven pairs of white braid across the chest. The white trousers are worn with black leather gaiters and heavy boots. The hat is similar to the Glengarry bonnet. The most closely comparable military uniform is the Light Dragoons of 1825.

In April 1920 Cecil Sharp arranged for the Handsworth Sword Dancers to dance in York for the EFDS vacation schools. Cecil Sharp was so pleased with the team's dancing that the EFDS awarded the team with a silver badge, the highest award that the Society could give at that time.

Because of this one of the dancers, Harry Siddell, made up the following poem:

THE DANCERS
by Joe Siddall

By the badge ye shall know them, for they wear it with pride,
These dancers of Handsworth who are famed far and wide;
For that badge is the symbol that they have stood the test
For many long years, and still are the best
Troupe of sword dancers to be found in the land;
And to see them in action – by gum, it is grand!
March, Clash, Snake, and Single Sword Up,
And in Three Divide they are just warming up.
Then quickly they slip into Double Sword Down,
A difficult figure that has won them renown.
And all through the figures they work like a clock,
And wind up the dance by making the Lock.
And the badges they wear are the locked swords, you see,
Presented to them by the E.F.D. Society
For the great display they gave at York,
Which for many days after was all the town's talk.
J H Siddall is the captain, and his brothers Joe, Walter and Will,
Along with Lomas, Barks and Staniforth, are dancers of skill,
And little Verdon, whose front name is Pat,
A neat little dancer as quick as a cat;
And the musician, by name Tommy Gray,
Who while they are dancing fine music does play.
And that's the full list of the dancers of note,
Who proudly carry the badge on their coat.

The Handsworth Sword Dancers
dancing around the Handsworth area
on their traditional date, Boxing Day.

GRENOSIDE SWORD DANCE

Cecil Sharp, the collector of English song and dance, was the man who started to give back to the English people their songs and dances.

In 1913 he visited Grenoside, again, like Handsworth, a stone's throw away from Sheffield. He wrote the following information about the dancers' costume.

"Six dancers and captain – all miners. Dancers dressed in close-fitting tunic of small pink patterned calico, with curious devices, all different, made of puckered red and blue braid covering back and front. Bows and rosettes of the same material dotted about. A red or blue – usually the former – frill of braid for collar. They wear white trousers, and the thing that is different to all the other traditional sword dancers is that they wear clogs.

When performing their dance, the dancers stand in two lines while the Captain walks up and down the passage, singing a song about the dancers. The dancers then form a circle and dance round. They make the lock and place this over the Captain's head. The dancers move round a bit faster and at the end of the phrase pull the sword out, therefore supposedly killing the Captain. The dance is then performed.

GRENOSIDE SWORD DANCE
by Peter Clarke

Each year, outside the pub on Boxing Day,
We stand, Christ-gentled,
Civilised,
Giving witness to the dance —
Tidy faces.
Petals on the Golden Bough
The tarmac shows us how to stand,
Rectangular, squaring the natural ring.
The swords are blunt,
The dancers shod in clogs,
The pretty costumes quaint.
The captain lies a brief moment in the wet,
His fox masking a pith-helmet.

These men who weave the endless chain
Web-close, within the crowd,
And knot their swords,
And slay their captain
Are linked
Sword-tip and sword-hilt,
Hand to hand and mouth to ear,
With all who ever dug their fingers
In the earth
And smelt the scent of green things
Growing —
With all who ever killed to eat
And fought to live
And felt their spittle thick for love —
With man —
With me.

I am not the single grain of sand,
The drop of water falling on the rock of time:
I bear my share by standing silent,
The ritual must be done
And watched.

Last year the dancers
Wove the sun and mist into a rainbow
Arching the village street.

The rough grain of the dance has been filled
With military polish:
Swords go with trumpets, soldiers
And the wounds of Cupid's darts.
Romantic bullshit.

The mystery has been
Coerced
Into what sense we make today
Of magic.

Why ask the meaning
Of rolling waves
As dancers arch and dive along the set —
    Seasons, furrows, reaping, weaving?

Of clashing swords —
    Fighting, threshing, sacrifice?
Of tinkling song,
Of endless chain,
Of god-king's death and resurrection —

Enough to sense
The depth of magic.
Animal spirits
Working in the dark
Linking us to timelessness
And binding us
To earth.

The Grenoside Sword Dancers dance on their traditional day – Boxing Day. They also dance on the Saturday about two weeks after the Boxing Day dance. This is called "the Village Traipse" where they dance farther afield outside of the village.

The Captain is dead!

GOATHLAND PLOUGH STOTS

"Stot" is the name for a bullock, and this name became transferred to the young man who pulled the plough in the procession on Plough Monday (the first Monday after Twelfth Night). This is what takes place at Goathland on Twelfth Night. The plough is wheeled into church to be blessed, and then the plough-crew would go round the village, visiting as many homes as possible, in the hope that those they visit will give them a gift, that is food or money. It is said that if the Plough Stots didn't receive anything they would plough up the garden of the offending house.

The following Saturday, the Plough Stots do their sword dance. They usually have two teams of six (sometimes three teams). They perform their dance in Goathland and then around other villages in the area. Their costume consists of team one in light pink long shirts with a white belt and dark trousers, and the other team wearing light blue long shirts with a white belt and dark trousers, with soft peak caps.

The Goathland Plough Stots were revived in 1923 and have gone on ever since, with the exception of the two world wars, up to 1950, and thankfully are still going strong.

As in other places, the locals maintain that the custom of the Plough being blessed and the sword dance goes back a thousand years to when the Norsemen settled in Yorkshire. This is brought about because the name Goathland is a derivative of Goder-land, meaning settlement of Norse Man.

There is sadly no evidence that says that the Plough Stots are that old. Never mind, so long as the sword dance continues for a long time to come, that is all that is needed.

T'OWLD 'OSS, RICHMOND

T'owld 'Oss, Richmond, 1895

The revival of T'owld 'Oss took place some years ago, and is now part of Richmond Christmas celebrations.

T'owld 'Oss and his attendants wander around the streets of Richmond calling at all the public houses, where the 'oss will be let loose amongst the drinkers, causing quite a lot of havoc. While this is going on the attendants sing the song "Poor Old Horse".

In the past the horse was accompanied by a fiddle, fife and drum, with a number of attendants, two of which were huntsmen, who carried long whips which they cracked throughout the song. In those days all of the T'owld 'Oss party blacked their faces, which of course is the best way to disguise oneself.

The head of the 'oss is a horse's skull with the mouth wired to let the person inside make the 'oss open and shut its mouth, which if done very fast would make a most frightening animal. The 'oss party performs their little ritual from Christmas Eve to New Year, visiting the pubs in the villages around Richmond.

POOR OLD HORSE

Come gentlemen and sportsmen,
And men of courage bold,
All you that's got a good old horse
Take care of him when old;
Go. put him in your stable,
And keep him there so warm,
Give him good corn and hay. Sir.
I'm sure he'll take no harm.
        Poor old horse, poor old horse.

Once I had my clothing
Of linsey-woolsey fine,
My tail and mane of length,
And my body it did shine,
But now I'm growing old. Sir,
And my nature does decay,
My master frowns upon me,
And thus I heard him say:
        Poor old horse, poor old horse.

These handsome little shoulders
That once were plump and round
They are decayed and drooped,
I fear they are not sound.
Also these little nimble legs
That oft ran many miles
Over hedges, over ditches
Over valleys, gates and stiles.
        Poor old horse, poor old horse.

Once I was young. Sir,
Aye and in my prime.
My master used to ride on me
And thought me very fine.
But now alas, it is not so
I've no such friends at all
I'm forced to nibble the short grass
That grows beneath yon wall.
           Poor old horse, poor old horse.

I used to be well tended
All in a stable warm.
To keep my tender body
From any cold or harm;
But now I'm turned adrift, Sir,
In the open fields to go,
To face all kinds of weather
Cold winds, and frost, and snow.
           Poor old horse, poor old horse.

TOLLING THE DEVIL'S KNELL, DEWSBURY

This custom takes place in All Saints Parish Church in Dewsbury. This is a large building, but the custom takes place in the small space that the bellringers use when they are pulling their bells. On Christmas Eve each year only one of the eight bells is rung, that is the tenor bell known as Black Tom of Soothill.

The legend is that a certain Sir Thomas du Soothill in the thirteenth century, out of rage, killed a servant. He was so upset about his horrid deed that he bought the tenor bell for the Parish Church which is known as the Black Tom of Soothill, and as it rang at Christmas it would remind Sir Thomas of his dastardly deed.

Black Tom is tolled the number of years since Jesus was born and is

Eighteenth-century ringers prepare for
Tolling the Devil's Knell: from a chap-book

so timed that the last toll strikes as midnight strokes, and that once again the Devil will stay away from Dewsbury. It is believed that when Christ was born the Devil died. While all this is going on there is a person sitting in the corner of the bellringers' chamber with a large board on his knees covered in white paper with a number of squares drawn so as to represent the number of

Dewsbury Minster

times the bell will be tolled, and as the bell strikes the person ticks off a square.

The old custom was discontinued at one time, but in 1928 it was revived. It was also discontinued through the war years, when the ringing of church bells was forbidden except as a signal of invasion.

The "Devil's Knell" did not escape the observant eye of the great ecclesiologist, Dr. Mule. In a collection of Christmas Carols published by him and Mr. Helmore in 1853 the following is found:

> Toll bell because there ends tonight
> An empire old and vast
> An empire of unquestioned right
>
> Toll
>
> Stretching wide from East'to West
> Ruling over every breast
> Each nation, tongue and caste.

Toll, toll because a monarch dies
Whom tyrant statutes ran
From polar snows to tropic skies
From Greenland to Japan

Toll

Crowded cities, lonely glens
Oceans, mountains, shores and fens
All called him Lord of Man.
Toll, toll because that monarch fought
Right fiercely for his own
And utmost craft and value brought
Before he was o'erthrown

Toll

He the lord and man the slave
His the kingdom of the grave
And all its dim unknown.

Joy, joy because a babe is born
Who after many a toil
The scorners' pride shall laugh to scorn
The work the toilers foil

Joy

God as you the earth hath tired
Therefore man shall be as God
And has the spoilers spoil.

It looks as though this charming little custom will continue for ever.

CANDLE AUCTION, HUMBERHOLME

Humberholme is a small village in North Yorkshire some distance north-east of Settle.

The name Humberholme suggests possible derivation from the Viking chieftain "Hubba" who is known to have had some authority in these parts.

When people who know nothing of customs hear that a Candle Auction is to take place, they think that it will be someone auctioning

candles. The Candle Auction that takes place at Humberholme is a far more serious event than just selling candles.

The George Inn is the building where the auction has always taken place, and the auction is for a piece of land that is situated between Humberholme and Raisgill, and is known as the "Poor Pastures" which is used for grazing sheep.

The Vicar is the auctioneer, the candle is lit at 8pm and the bidding starts. At the beginning it is not taken very seriously and it is a bit of a pantomime, but as the candle burns down then it becomes a very serious matter. The last bid as the candle goes out is the person who will be able to use the "Poor Pastures."

The Candle Auction is known by some of the locals as the "Parliament", the Vicar and his Wardens as the "House of Lords" and the Bidders are the House of Commons. It is not known who started this little custom or who owned the land that is bid for. In the past the money that was made used to be given to the poor of the Parish. Nowadays the money is distributed among the needy in the village. Food, toys, clothing and other necessities are given

For some people it is felt that the charity goes back at least 200 years, and it looks as though it is safe to go on for another 200 years, on New Year's Eve,

Although the Custom is small compared to some it still is a very good event and means a lot to the farmers in the area, and as someone said, "It's a good social evening."

Moveable Feasts

The Horn Blower, Ripon

The Horn Blower of Ripon is a very dedicated man, in that he has to blow the horn every evening of the year, including Christmas Day, New Year's Eve, etc. There is no let-up.

There are not many customs in this country that are as old as this one. The horn has been blown in Ripon without a break since Alfred the Great's Charter of Incorporation as a Royal Borough in 886.

The Horn Blower performs his little ceremony every evening at 9pm by blowing his horn on each corner of the market cross, and having done that he then goes to the present Mayor's House and gives

one blow to let the Mayor know that he has done his duty.

Originally this was to "set the watch", after which, if any premises were robbed before sunrise, the sufferer received compensation for his loss from an annual tax based on the number of doors a householder had. That was for two doors 4d. a year and one door 2d. This tax, a very early insurance, fell into disuse, but the traditional blowing still takes place.

Maybe another reason for the horn being blown was a curfew, and anyone found on the streets after the horn had been blown could find themselves in the local "lock-up".

The city has four horns, the oldest being the Charter Horn, which is supposed to go back to 886. The second horn, now used as a reserve, was acquired in 1690, and the third Horn, purchased by the Mayor in 1865. A fourth horn was given to the city in the year 1886, which came from Chillingham herd of wild cattle in Northumberland. The Horn and Charter Horn are both on display in the Town Hall, on application.

HORN BLOWING, BAINBRIDGE

Bainbridge is a small village just south of Askrigg in North Yorkshire. The present horn was given to the village in 1864. It is a buffalo horn, and it replaces the bullock horn which used to be blown.

The horn is blown in the village main street at 9pm each evening, but not the whole year round. Officially the horn should be blown from late September until the end of March. These are the darker days of the year, so the horn blower can be much appreciated by any persons who are lost on the moor, and the sound will help them to find their way to civilisation. That is why the horn is blown, according to tradition, and it has been blown for many hundreds of years – some say seven hundred years.

For many generations the family that has been deeply involved with horn blowing is the Metcalfe family. The family is extremely old. James Metcalfe, who it seems was the founder of the Metcalfes, was well known for his rule of the dale, and he returned from the French campaign a rich man in 1415, and was made Chief Forester of Wensleydale. When Sir Christopher Metcalfe was made High Sheriff of York in 1555, he rode to his appointment at the head of three hundred Metcalfes, each riding a white horse.

In 1983 Alistair Metcalfe was eleven years old and the next in line to blow the horn. That was after his great-uncle Jack Metcalfe died, which ended a 36-year reign as Bainbridge's Horn Blower. If you want to know when the custom started, you will get several answers. "The Romans started it," is one, and in fact the Romans did visit Bainbridge and built a fort known as Visoridum,

Traces can be seen on a mound east of the village. Another answer is that the whole thing was started by William the Conqueror. A more likely story is that it was the local monks who blew a horn to guide

folk over the fells when the dark weather began.

There is the story that a certain James Metcalfe, who was the Horn Blower after the Second World War, went to Askrigg one day and was talking to his friends there when he heard the clock strike 9.30 pm. He had lost count of the time and dashed back to Bainbridge. He got the horn and gave three loud blasts (not too loud). When he got home, "Well," said his wife when he went into the kitchen, "what about t'Horn?" "It's late," he said, "but I've blown it." His wife then said, "They've had a double dose tonight then. Our George blew it at nine o'clock."

The Horn of Ulphas

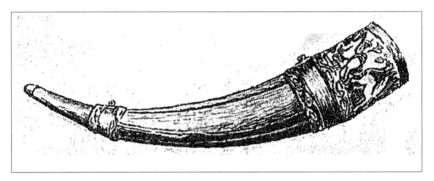

The Horn of Ulphus is made of ivory, now mellowed with age, twenty-one and a half inches in length with a diameter at the larger end of five inches. At the end there is a band of carvings. We see a gryphon (Apollo, the Sun) confronted by a chimera (Winter and Tempest). Between there is planted the Tree of Life with fifteen leaves (Period of the Full Moon). The other creatures are a Unicorn (Taurus, zodiacal sign of the first month of Spring) and Leo (the Summer Solstice) again with a Tree of Life.

Could this therefore be a Horn of Ceremony maybe of Mesopotamian origin and of the tenth century, used for very important religious ceremonies? It could have found its way, by well-known overland routes via Russia, Poland and Denmark, into the hands of King Canute in the eleventh century. Canute was elected King of England in AD1016 and King of Denmark in 1019.

Ulp was one of the foremost of King Canute's men, and between 1016 and 1026 had become owner of much land between the Humber and the Tees.

How did the Ulph Horn eventually become the property of the York

Minster? The story/legend goes that after his eldest son Adelbert was killed in battle, Ulph attempted to bypass the claims of his three sons and bequeath his domain to Adelbert's daughter Adelwynne. She however persuaded him to bestow his lands on the Church. Accordingly Ulph rode to York, taking with him his largest drinking horn. Filling it with wine, he knelt at the high altar in York Minster and, drinking off the wine, laid the Horn on the altar to be held by the church for all time as title to the lands over which he held sway and to all his wealth.

This is possibly just a story, because in 1028 or 1029 Ulph was found guilty of treason and was murdered by order of King Canute. It is therefore reasonable to suppose that his lands were confiscated by the King. So it would follow that the horn was given as a gift from Canute to the Minster.

The Horn of Ulphus is still to be found in York Minster.

Detail of carving, drawn by Miss H. L. Hodgson

DENBY DALE PIE

Denby Dale lies a few miles to the west of Barnsley. The Great Pie of Denby Dale has over the years grown bigger and bigger each time it is baked. The pie-making is not an annual affair, it is made to celebrate special events.

The latest pie to be baked was in the year 2000 to celebrate the coming of the Millennium, and it was the tenth pie to be baked.

The first pie was made in 1788 to celebrate the recovery of King George III from mental illness. There are however some local historians and folklorists who say the pie was baked long before that date, but there is no evidence. Here are the years when the local people produced a great pie:

1815 to commemorate the Battle of Waterloo
1846 to celebrate the repeal of the Corn Laws
1887 to celebrate Queen Victoria's Golden Jubilee.
    (The pie had bad meat in it, which made it uneatable.)
1887 One week after the disaster, another pie was baked which
    proved to be very eatable. This was known as the
    "Resurrection Pie".
1896 The 50th anniversary of the repeal of the Corn Laws
1928 To raise money for the Huddersfield Royal Infirmary
1964 To celebrate the birth of four royal babies, all born in the
    same year
1988 Celebrating 100 years of the Denby Dale Pie
2000 The Millennium

The village did not celebrate the ending of two world wars, due to the lack of ingredients. Because of rationing, they couldn't even make a

small pie, let alone a giant one.

The 2000 Millennium Pie was the biggest yet, and it keeps its name in the Guinness Book of Records.

To show how big the pie was:

The pie weighed in at 12 tonnes, being 12 metres (40 feet) long, 2·5 metres (8 feet) wide and 1·1 metres (44 inches) deep.

The ingredients were:

> 5000 kg diced prime British beef
> 2000 kg potatoes
> 1000 kg onions
> 3900 kg water
> 100 kg "John Smith" best bitter
> 200 kg beef bouillon, mixed herbs and gravy
> Salt and pepper to taste
> 3465 kg short crust pastry

It is not just the pie that takes place at Denby Dale, but a whole day of entertainment with an arena and a separate stage. It is a full weekend of activities plus a fun fair.

At 12.30pm on the Saturday the Great Pie is in procession from the Dalesman Public House to the field where all the fun is taking place. The procession includes the local majorettes, local bands, scouts and cubs, stilt walkers, jazzmen, etc. When the Pie arrives at the field it is blessed by the Bishop of Wakefield. Then the distribution takes place. First sitting is served to yellow ticket holders, the second sitting is served to blue ticket holders and the third sitting to green ticket holders. After the green ticket session, thousands and thousands of people have been fed. The serving has now been completed, and all we have to do is wait for another bigger Giant Pie to be made. But when will that be?

The Stunning Great
MEAT PIE

A proper and pious ditty,
to be taken with a peck of salt.

You've heard of the wondrous crocodile,
And the thundering great sea snake,
No doubt it's often made you smile,
And caused your sides to ache;
Now I've. got one that'll make you laugh
For a month to come, or nigh -
So listen while I tell you about
A stunning great rneat pie.

Now hungry folk can eat a horse -
So I hope you'll swallow this tale,
Of the thirty-thousand-portion, pie
Cooked up in Denby Dale;

You may guess it was a tidy size,
It took a week to make it;
A day to carry it to the shop,
And just a week to bake it.   .
Oh: had you seen it, I'll be bound,
Your wonder you'd scarce govern;
They were forced to break the front wall down
to get it to the oven.

It took full thirty sacks of flour,
It's a fact now that I utter,

Three hundred pails of water too,
And a hundred tubs of butter.
The crust was nearly seven feet thick,
You couldn't easy bruise it;
And the rolling pin was such a size
That it took twelve men to use it;

There were twenty-five spare-ribs of pork,
I'm sure I'm not mistaken;
With two-and-thirty hams from York,
And twenty sides of bacon.
The pie was made by fifty cooks -
And all of them first raters' -
And then they filled up all the nooks
With a ton of kidney taters;

When word was given a general rush
Took place to hack and hew it;
They clambered up outside the crust
To get their knives into it,
When all at once the crust gave way,
It's true, I'll take my davy:
And ninety-five poor souls, they say,
Were drowned in the gravy!

125

Compiled by Martin Shaw, 1915

EASTER

WILLIAM TUFTON DOLE, PENISTONE, SHEFFIELD

Penistone is north-west of Sheffield, but Barnsley is nearer on the south-east side.

In 1559 a William Tufton gave one quarter of rye to the poor of Penistone to be distributed on the morning of Good Friday each year. The rye was rendered by the persons in occupation of the estate situated at Hexley in the parish of Denby, and was brought into the porch of Penistone Parish Church and distributed there and then by the assistant overseer to the poor of the parish.

Some years ago the custom was revived, and at that time the sum of £3.4.0d. was received annually from the Charity Commissioners by the Penistone Urban District Council and was spent on ordinary flour, which is distributed by the Clerk to the Council at 10.30am on the steps of the Town Hall on Good Friday.

The recipients are mainly children, with a few adults. Their attendance is more by habit than by poverty. It is good to see that quite a number of older people attend, who were in their youth, receivers of the dole. The £3.4.0d. has now become £3.20p.

Sadly over the past few years the numbers have dwindled, but even when it was suggested that small charities should merge, the Penistone Council requested that this one should be retained.

SHIPLEY HORSE FAIR

The horse fair in Shipley has been in existence since 1753, but this date is only because at that time it was a well-established fair. It is of course much older than that, in fact no-one knows how far back the horse fair goes.

The fair takes place each year on Easter Tuesday, and has gone through many changes. In particular the venue has changed a number of times, and over the years the numbers attending have dropped, likewise the number of horses has fallen greatly, but they still continue with this community's traditional horse fair.

The 1950's, in particular 1952, saw the fair at its peak, with thousands coming to see the sale of horses, and over 200 horses with their owners. When a purchase had taken place the slap of a hand-shake would clinch the deal.

The newspapers have been reporting that the crowds have reduced each year, and they report that the Shipley horse fair is destined not to take place next year, but each year there is enough Gypsy attendance

to make it worthwhile. As always, there are enough people to meet and talk about horses, walk through the horse muck and buy and sell horses. According to one resident, "This is more an unofficial fair," but it still continues.

SAMUEL JOBSON BREAD CHARITY, SOUTH CAVE
HUMBERSIDE

South Cave is around twenty-five miles west of Kingston Upon Hull. The charity is involved with South Cave, Broomfleet and Flaxfleet.

Samuel Jobson was a regular church-goer and very much a God-fearing man. He was baptised in 1623 in All Saints Church, South Cave, and buried in the church in 1687. The Charity didn't start until 1697.

He left in his will money and a cottage and land in Brankingham to the Churchwardens (unusual, it is usually the Vicar) of South Cave, on condition that they pay one pound a year for an anniversary sermon preached on the Tuesday after Easter, to be followed immediately by the distribution of white bread to the poor. Today a white loaf of bread is a normal loaf, so it is taken for granted, but back in the 1600s it was very much a delicacy because the normal bread in those days was a very unpalatable rye bread, so it would seem that the poor and disadvantaged of South Cave looked forward to the Tuesday after Easter. So every Tuesday after Easter a service was held and the local vicar sermonised on the Samuel Jobson Bread Charity, to remember him and let the congregation hear all about this very generous man. It was and still is known as the Samuel Jobson Bread Service. Over the years the charity has been looked after by Trustees. In 1883 the Charity Commissioners decided that the charity should be extended to the poor and disadvantaged of Broomfleet and Flaxfleet. There is also another payment at Christmas time when the elderly are given a small amount of money, which is appreciated by all.

As mentioned before, Samuel Jobson was a God-fearing man, in fact the extract below is found at the beginning of his will:

"First and principally I bequeath my soul into the protection of my Lord and Saviour Jesus Christ, by whose meritorious death and precious blood-shedding I hope to have full and free pardon and remission of my sins and inherit everlasting life."

EGG ROLLING

From pre-Christian times the egg has always been a symbol of life, and is used at Easter to symbolise the resurrection of Christ.

Throughout England there are many customs associated with the egg. For instance, in County Durham the children still play the game of "Jopping", that is the egg is held in the hand with just a small part showing between the thumb and the index finger. You "jop" by knocking the bit of egg showing, and if it doesn't break then that is the winner. The eggs are hard-boiled, of course.

Then there is "Egg Shackling" as performed in the primary schools in Somerset. The eggs are put into a large sieve and they are "shackled" by the teacher moving the sieve forward and backward. As the eggs start to crack, they are taken out, and the one that remains unbroken is, of course, the winner.

The most popular egg custom is "Egg Rolling" and this is enacted all over the country. There are a couple of Egg Rolling Customs in Yorkshire.

FOUNTAINS ABBEY

Easter Monday is the day that the Rolling takes place. This was revived after the National Trust bought the estate, and was suggested by an estate worker who remembered it from his boyhood; this was in 1984. The hard-boiled eggs are rolled down a bank by the side of the Abbey. The children are divided into three groups, and the three eggs furthest down the hill for each group wins a prize.

HOYLAND, near Barnsley

There is evidence that Egg Rolling had been an Easter activity, but the local school has a hill nearby, so it was thought that egg rolling might

brighten up the Easter celebrations. The children in the Junior and Infant School decorate their eggs, which are judged for best pattern, etc. After the judging the whole school go to the nearby hill and each class rolls their eggs in turn.

PACE EGGING PLAY

The play is slightly different to the other plays in England. They have the usual fight between George/St. George, (King George and the Valiant Soldier/Slasher/ the valiant soldier, is killed after a fight with swords. Then the Doctor is called and with a bit of fooling the soldier is brought back to life. Then there is another fight between St. George and the Black Prince of Paradine. The Black Prince is slain. The King of Egypt now appears asking for his son, the Black Prince of Paradine. Finding out that his precious son is dead, he calls in Hector to deal with St. George, Hector and St. George fight, and Hector is wounded. At this point an odd character appears, that of Toss Pot. The play finishes with the traditional Pace Egg song.

They all then move off to another pitch to enact the play once more.

The costume worn in Midgley is a pink smock with coloured paper rosettes. Brighouse has the same costume, only white smocks are worn. The doctor, however, is dressed in a black suit and wearing a top hat. Both teams wear the same headgear, that is a square mortarboard with a May garland that is cut in half and placed upon the board, with streamers attached to the board and coming down to hide the face.

Both teams perform their play over the Easter period. To find out the times and the places they are performing at, it's best to contact the local Tourist

Information Centre or the local council.

THE PACE EGG PLAY

Pace Egg is a corruption of "Pasch Egg" and the Latin Pascha meaning Easter.

The Pace Egg Play is found in Yorkshire and Lancashire and, as the title conveys, it is performed at Easter time.

England is very lucky in that it has a few other sorts of ritual drama. For instance the Mumming Play is found all over England and it is performed at Christmas. Then there is the Plough Play, performed on Plough Monday and the days after (Plough Monday is the Monday after 12th Day). Then there are the Plough Jays performing on Plough Monday. This set of plays takes place in Nottingham, Leicestershire and Lincolnshire. Then at Easter there is the Pace Egg Play, and around All Souls (31st October to 1st November) the Soul Caking Play performed mainly in Cheshire.

There are only two Pace Egging Plays being performed traditionally in Yorkshire – one at Midgley and the other at Brighouse. These two places are situated right in the middle of the industrial part of West Yorkshire, very near to Wakefield, Huddersfield and Dewsbury. The two teams have been performing their Pace Egging Plays for many years now.

Midgley Pace Eggers

Brighouse Pace Eggers

THE

PEACE EGG.

PRINTED FOR
THE TROUBADOUR
BY JOHN FOREMAN
BROADSHEET KING

THE PEACE EGG.

ACT I.

Enter Actors.

Fool.—Room, room, Brave gallants, give us room
    to sport,
For in this room we wish for to resort,
Resort, and to repeat you our merry rhyme,
For remember, good sirs, this is Christmas time.
The time to cut up goose-pies now doth appear,
So we are come to act our merry Christmas here,
At the sound of the trumpet, and beat of the drum,
Make room, brave gentlemen, and let our actors come,
We are the merry actors that traverse the street;

THE PEACE EGG. 3

We are the merry actors that fight for our meat,
We are the merry actors that show pleasant play,
Step in, St. George, thou champion, and clear the way.

Enter St. George.

I am St. George, who from old England sprung;
My famous name throughout the world hath rung,
Many bloody deeds and wonders have I made known,
And made the tyrants tremble on their throne.
I followed a fair lady to a giant's gate,
Confined in dungeon deep to meet her fate;
Then I resolved with true knight-errantry,
To burst the door, and set the prisoner free,
When a giant almost struck me dead,
But by my valour I cut off his head.

140

4.   THE PEACE EGG.

I've searched the word all round and round,
But a man to equal me I never found.

Enter Slasher to St. George.

Slasher.—I am a valiant soldier, and Slasher is my
    name,
With sword and buckler by my side I hope to win
    the game.
And for to fight with me I see thou art not able,
So with my trusty broad-sword I soon will thee
    disable.

St. George.—Disable! disable! it lies not in thy
    power,
For with my glittering sword and spear I soon will
    thee devour.
Stand off! Slasher! let no more be said,
For if I draw my sword I'm sure to break thy head.

Slasher.—How canst thou break my head?
Since it is made of iron,
And my body's made of steel,
My hands and feet of knuckle bone,
I challenge thee to field.—*(They fight, and Slasher is
    wounded. Exit St. George.)*

Enter Fool to Slasher.

Fool.—Alas! alas! my chiefest son is slain,
What must I do to raise him up again?
Here he lies in the presence of you all;
I'll lovingly for a doctor call.
(Aloud) A doctor! a doctor! ten pounds for a doctor.
I'll go and fetch a doctor. *(Going.)*

Enter Doctor.

Doctor.—Here am I.
Fool.—Are you the doctor?
Doctor.—Yes; that you may plainly see, by my
    art and activity.
Fool.—Well, what's your fee to cure this man?
Doctor.—Ten pounds is my fee: but Jack, if thou
be an honest man, I'll only take five of thee.

Fool. (Aside.) You'll be wondrous cunning if you get any.

Well, how far have you travelled in doctrineship?

Doctor.—From Italy, Titaly, High Germany, France and Spain, and now am returned to cure the diseases in Old England again.

Fool.—So far, and no further.

Doctor.—O yes! a great deal further.

Fool.—How far?

Doctor.—From the fireside cupboard, upstairs, and into bed.

Fool.—What diseases can you cure?

Doctor.—All sorts.

Fool.—What's all sorts?

Doctor.—The itch, the stitch, the palsy and the gout. If a man gets nineteen devils in his skull, I'll cast twenty of them out. I have in my pockets, crutches for lame ducks, spectacles for blind humble-bees, packsaddles and panniers for grasshoppers, and plaisters for broken-backed mice. I cured Sir Harry of a nang-nail, almost fifty-five yards long, surely I can cure this poor man.—Here, Jack, take a little out of my bottle, and let it run down thy throttle; if thou be not quite slain, rise, Jack, and fight again.

(Slasher rises.)

Slasher.—O my back.

Fool.—What's amiss with thy back?

Slasher.—My back it is wounded,

And my heart is confounded,

To be struck out of seven senses into four-score,

The like was never seen in Old England before.

Enter St. George.

O hark! St. George, I hear the silver trumpet sound,

That summons us from off this bloody ground;

Farewell, St. George, we can no longer stay.

Down yonder is the way. *(Pointing.)*

Exit Slasher, Doctor, and Fool.

6   THE PEACE EGG.

ACT II.

St. Geo.—I am St. George, that noble champion bold,
And with my trusty sword I won ten thousand pounds
    in gold;
'Twas I that fought the fiery dragon, and brought
    him to the slaughter,
And by those means I won the King of Egypt's
    daughter.

Enter Prince of Paradine.

Prince.—I am Black Prince of Paradine, born of
    high renown;
Soon I will fetch St. George's lofty courage down!
Before St. George shall be received by me,
St. George shall die to all eternity.

St. George.—Stand off, thou black Morocco dog,
Or by my sword thou'lt die,
I'll pierce thy body full of holes, and make thy
    buttons fly.

Prince.—Draw out thy sword and slay.
Pull out thy purse and pay,
For I will have a recompense,
Before I go away.

St. George.—Now Prince of Paradine, where have
    you been,
And what fine sights pray have you seen,
Dost think that no man of thy age,
Dares such a black as thee engage?
Lay down thy sword, take up to me a spear,
And then I'll fight thee without dread or fear. *(They
    fight, and Prince of Paradine is slain.)*

St George.—Now Prince of Paradine is dead,
And all his joys entirely fled,
Take him and give him to the flies,
Let him no more come near my eyes.

Enter King of Egypt.

King.—I am the King of Egypt, as plainly doth
    appear,

143

I'm come to seek my son, my son and only heir.
St. George.—He is slain.
King.—Who did him slay, who did him kill,
    And on the ground his precious blood did spill?
St. George.—I did him slay, I did him kill,
And on the ground his precious blood did spill.
Please you, my liege, my honour to maintain,
Had you been there you might have fared the same.
    King.—Cursed Christian! what is this thou'st done?
Thou hast ruined me, and slain my only son.
    St. Geo.—He gave me a challenge, who now it denies?
How high he was, but see how low he lies!
    King.—O Hector! Hector! help me with speed,
For in my life I never stood more need.

Enter Hector.

And stand not there with sword in hand,
But rise and fight at my command.
    Hector.—Yes, yes, my liege, I will obey,
And by my sword I hope to win the day;
If that be he who doth stand there,
That slew my master's son and heir,
If he be sprung from royal blood,
I'll make it run like Noah's flood.
    St. George.—Hold, Hector! do not be so hot,
For here thou know'st not who thou'st got,
For I can tame thee of thy pride,
And lay thine anger, too, aside;
Inch thee, and cut thee as small as flies,
And send thee over the sea to make mince-pies,
Mince pies hot, and mince pies cold,
I'll send thee to Black Sam before thou'rt three days old.
    Hector.—How canst thou tame me of my pride,
And lay mine anger too aside,
Inch me, and cut me as small as flies,
Send me over the sea to make mince pies,
Mince pies hot, and mince pies cold,
How canst thou send me to Black Sam before I'm
    three days old?

Since my head is made of iron,
My body's made of steel,
My hands and feet of knuckle bone,
I challenge thee to field.   *(They fight and Hector is
    wounded.)*
I am a valiant knight, and Hector is my name,
Many bloody battles have I fought, and always won
    the same,
But from St. George I received this bloody wound.
    (A trumpet sounds.)
Hark! hark! I hear the silver trumpet sound,
Down yonder is the way, *(pointing,)*
Farewell, St. George, I can no longer stay.   *(Exit.)*

Enter Fool to St George.

St. *George.*—Here comes from post, old Bold Ben.
Fool.—Why, master, did ever I take you to be my
    friend?
St. *Geo.*—Why, Jack, did ever I do thee any harm?
Fool.—Thou proud saucy coxcomb, begone!
St. *George.*—A coxcomb, I defy that name!
With a sword thou ought to be stabbed for the same.
Fool.—To be stabbed is the least I fear,
Appoint your time and place, I'll meet you there.
St. *George.*—I'll cross the water at the hour of five,
And meet you there, Sir, if I be alive.   *(Exit.)*

Enter Beelzebub.

Here come I Beelzebub,
And over my shoulders I carry my club,
And in my hand a dripping pan,
And I think myself a jolly old man,
And if you don't believe what I say,
Enter in Devil Doubt, and clear the way.

Enter Devil Doubt.

Here come I, little Devil Doubt,
If you do not give me money I'll sweep you all out;
Money I want and money I crave,
If you do not give me money, I'll sweep you all to the
    grave.

THE WORLD COAL CARRYING CHAMPIONSHIP

Gawthorpe is a small village on the outskirts of Wakefield, and is best known for its maypole and its celebrations on their May Festival. Interestingly the maypole committee organises the World Coal Carrying Championship. The Maypole is a very old tradition and the Coal Carrying was only started in 1963. Therefore according to the experts it isn't a custom, but because the championship involves the whole village and everyone is connected somehow with the championship, it really does make it a custom. There is a rather interesting way in which the coal carrying championship started.

It seems that one day in 1963 in the old pub of the Beehive, Reggie Sedgewick and Amos Chapman, a local coal merchant and president of the maypole committee, were enjoying some well-earned liquid refreshment while stood at the bar deep in thought, when in burst one

Lewis Hortley in a somewhat exuberant mood. On seeing the other two he said to Reggie, "Ba gum, lad, tha' looks buggered," slapping Reggie heartily on the back. Whether because of the force of the blow or because of the words that accompanied it, Reggie was just a little bit put out. "Ah'm as fit as thee," he told Lewis, "an' if tha' don't believe me, gerra bagga coil (coal) on thi back, ah'll get one on mine, an'll race thee to the top o't wood." Before Lewis had time to think about the challenge, Mr. Fred Hirst, who was

secretary to the maypole committee, raised a cautionary hand. "Old on a minute," said Fred. "'Aven't we been looking for something to do on Easter Monday. If we're gonna 'ave a race, let's 'ave it then. Let's 'ave a coil race from Barracks to Maypole," (the Barracks being the more common name given by the locals to the Royal Oak Public House).

So from that meeting and discussion the Gawthorpe World Coal Carrying Championship was born, and has been held every Easter Monday from that meeting.

The Championship in the early days attracted a crowd, but now the attraction embraces an extremely large crowd from all over Yorkshire and further afield.

GAWTHORPE MAYPOLE COMMITTEE
ESTABLISHED 1874
Secretary Mr. Brian Wilding   Treasurer Mrs. Susan Walshaw

THE WORLD COAL CARRYING
CHAMPIONSHIP

SPONSORED BY H.B.CLARK'S (SUCCESSOR'S)

WESTGATE BREWERY. WAKEFIELD

EASTER MONDAY

Starting around noon at the Royal Oak public house on Owl Lane, Gawthorpe and finishing at The Maypole on the village green.
The Current World Records are.
4 mins. 6 secs. (Men)   5 mins. 5 secs. (Ladies)

Gawthorpe is a small village situated on the outskirts of Ossett, Nr. Wakefield in Yorkshire. Parking is available within the area of the village and the actual race.

THE WORLD COAL CARRYING CONTEST.

148

The main event is the Men's Race, starting at The Royal Oak, Owl Lane, from where the competitors have to run, carrying a bag of coal weighing one hundredweight (50 kg) for close on a mile 11·08 yards (1012·5 metres) towards the Maypole on the village green, and when getting there the bag of coal is dropped at the base of the Pole. The Men's Championship record is 4 minutes 6 seconds, held by David Jones of Meltham. This is the second time that Mr. Jones has achieved this timing.

In the early days the Ladies' Race was not so far to run, racing from the bottom of the village to the Maypole. Now the ladies run the same course as the men. The ladies' bag of coal weighs 25 pounds (10 kg). The World Ladies' Champion is Julia Knight of Meltham, running the course in 5 minutes 5 seconds.

It seems that sometime in the 1960's it was proposed to hold a rolling-pin throwing contest, but luckily this never came to anything. In 1999 the committee decided to hold children's races, Under 9s, Under 11s and Under 15s.

The whole event is sponsored by the local Brewers H. B. Clark's of Wakefield, also the Solid Fuel Advisory Service supply vouchers and there may even be free holidays. The two World Champions receive a Trophy and a Tankard.

No event in the Olympic Games could stimulate more enthusiasm than this annual contest of stamina and muscle.

149

Tower Top Singing, Beverley and Baildon

The singing from the top of church towers is not only done in Yorkshire. The most famous one, of course, is the singing from the tower of Magdalen College, Oxford, and on the top of Bargate,

Beverley Minster

Southampton. The Oxford singing goes back many hundred years.

But why Beverley Minster? It seems that the choirmaster of Beverley thought it would be a good idea to get the choirboys up to the West Tower on Easter Day and sing a couple of Easter hymns, usually:

Jesus Christ is risen today – Alleluia

Our triumphant holy day – Alleluia

He had the idea in 1876, and that is when the first Tower Top singing started. No-one knows why he had this idea; it could well have been that the choirmaster was inspired by the May Day singing in Oxford.

It is not known how the singing first started, but there is a theory that a Requiem Mass for Henry VII used to be sung on the Tower Top on May 1st, and that when the practice ceased at the Reformation the present custom was substituted for it. However, there is no real evidence for this story.

The weather at Easter time is really very unpredictable, and there have been years when it has been pouring down with rain, or it was snowing, or the wind was so fierce that those beneath the tower could not hear the singing. Because of these problems the choirmaster in 1976 suggested that it might be a good idea to stop the custom, but the public would not allow it. So the Beverley Tower Top Singing still remains with us.

BAILDON TOWER TOP SINGING

Baildon is a few miles north of Bradford, and on Ascension Day the choir climb to the top of St. John's church tower and sing a hymn. After the one hymn the choir returns to ground level and continues with an open air service. The Vicar at that time had previously been a minor canon at Canterbury Cathedral, and thought it would be a good idea to bring the same custom to Baildon, which he did very successfully.

SPRING BANK HOLIDAY

BELLERBY GUISERS

Sadly this custom no longer takes place, and as seen in this book, it deals with customs that are still taking place. The reason that Bellerby is included is because it has just stopped but it is such an interesting custom that it should be part of this book.

Within recent years the custom started early, the pub opening at 7am and the women of the village helping the men to dress. The older men dressed as clowns, the younger men as females. The women also put the make-up on the men. Those acting as women were heavily made-up with lots of red on the lips. The reason for that is that if the

young men caught a woman they would give them a big sloppy kiss, leaving the woman with large red smudged lips. As soon as the young men "females" are fully dressed and made up, they then go out on to the main road and stop all cars that come along, asking for money.

At 11am the whole crew start to walk around the village with a large pan, led by a melodeon player and a drum. The carriers of the large pan visit each house in the village to collect food and money. The collection is brought to a place in the village, and the food is laid out on tables so that the children of the village have a good old "bun fight".

This is a prime example of how a custom can deteriorate, in that the Bellerby Guisers at one time would have come out at Christmas time, because the village had a sword dance and a mumming play attached. Some of the characters in the play are clowns, hence the clowns. The sword dancers wore rosettes and short ribbons, hence those wearing streamers of recent years. Over the years the custom has become just the collection of food and money, and the date has changed from Christmas to Whit Monday.

THE BRADFORD WHIT WALK

The walk used to take place on Whit Monday, and when it was decided to do away with Whit Monday as a bank holiday and introduce the Spring Bank Holiday, it was decided to move the walk to the latter. Whit was dropped from the title of the walk, but because there was such a large protest, they have put back the Whit, so it is the Bradford Whit Walk.

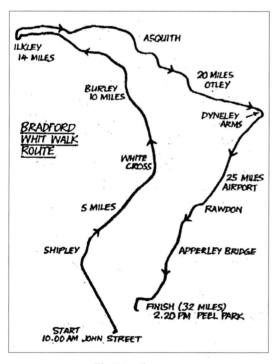

The 32-mile course

The first walk was held in 1903 and it was from Bradford to York, thirty-nine and a half miles. This was the route for three years, starting time 6am. In 1906 the walk became a circular route of forty and a half miles with a little later start time of 7.45am. At this stage the walk was thrown open to all comers. Previously it was only local workers that could take part.

The circular route started from Bradford via Ilkley and Bolton Abbey, and back through Ilkley, Otley and Bradford. That remained the route up until the 1914-18 war; the walk continued through the war years. In 1915 the distance dropped from forty and a half to thirty-two and a half miles. During the 1939-45 war the distance changed again, down to fifteen and a half miles. Then in 1948 came the biggest change when instead of thirty-two and a half miles it became fifty kilometres (31 miles 121 yards).

Quite a number of the walkers have won the race more than once. A certain Albert Johnson of Sheffield came first nine times between 1954 and 1963. He was the youngest winner at 23 years old. In 1919 he had been leading all the way, but as he left Otley he was overtaken, and at that moment he collapsed on the grass verge.

Ambulance men attended to him, and minutes later he was up and off once more, gathering strength as he went forward. He was fortified by three double brandies set up for him at pubs along the route by one of the timekeepers.

The start of the first Bradford Whit Walk 1903

It is interesting to note that when the walk first started in 1903 it was the first long-distance road walk in Britain as an open event for amateurs.

Although the attendance of the walkers and spectators has decreased over the years, the enthusiasm of the people of Bradford will make sure it continues. "The Bradford" is the name of the walk by the locals. It is worth a trip to see "The Bradford", which is still very exciting.

CARLIN SUNDAY

Carlin Sunday is Passion Sunday in the Christian calendar, which is the fifth Sunday in Lent.

Carlin Sunday is recognised at Hull in East Yorkshire and Newcastle upon Tyne. This is because Yorkshire has a story about how Carlin Sunday came about, likewise Tyneside has a similar story.

The Yorkshire story goes that well over 100 years ago on the fifth Sunday in Lent, a ship carrying a cargo of peas was shipwrecked in bad weather off Hunmanby Gap in Filey Bay. The peas were dried peas, so that when they came into contact with the sea water they swelled up, and the women each took a large amount and boiled them. The population around Filey was at that time a starving community, so it was as if God had sent the ship for them so that they would no longer be hungry.

The Tyneside version is that the ship, loaded with peas, arrived at Newcastle and docked on the river Tyne. A rather heavy storm arrived and the ship had already docked, so that the ship and crew were safe. They celebrated their safe arrival by cooking the peas. At that time the population, like at Filey, were starving, and they prayed that something should be sent to them to satisfy their hunger. And, the story goes, food did arrive.

According to legend the ship was named Carting, and in some cases the ship's captain was called Carling. And that is the reason why we eat carlins in the north-east of England.

Children used to say the following:

> Tia, Mid, Micern, Carlin,
> Patey, Pace Egg Day,
> All these are the Sundays for Easter.

Soak the carlins (Grey Peas) in water overnight
Drain off the water and add bicarbonate of soda (just a pinch)
Likewise salt and sugar. Boil until soft.
In some cases boil until the peas become mushy.

There are still a number of pubs that put plates of Carlins on the bar
for their customers on Carlin Sunday.

SHROVETIDE

SKIPPING FESTIVAL, SCARBOROUGH

This custom takes place on the Promenade on Shrove Tuesday each year, when the whole of Scarborough congregate on the sea front, and everyone, old and young alike, gets hold of a rope and skips. It may be just one person skipping or five or six at the same time under one rope.

It is said that this event has been going on for hundreds of years. According to contemporary records, however, it did not start until the early 1900's.

Thomas Hinderwell, who wrote his *History of Scarborough* at the end of the 19th century, made no mention of Shrove Tuesday skipping. Neither did Joseph Brogden who wrote a *History of Scarborough* in 1881/82 after a two-year appeal to aged Scarborians for information about local Customs and Folklore. Surely if the custom had been performed for hundreds of years these two well-known local historians

would have at least mentioned the Shrove Tuesday skipping.

So if the skipping didn't originate until the 1900's, what was going on along the sea front before this? According to the older generation, Shrove Tuesday was known as "Ball Day" and it was a day when the town's apprentices, servants and school children had a half-day holiday, and they all assembled on the South Sands and played many different types of ball games. The balls, made of cloth stuffed with sawdust, were on sale at local Scarborough shops. It seems that on Shrove Tuesday the South Sands resembled a country fair with stalls, booths, hawkers selling pies, buns, gingerbread men, sweets, fruit and cloth balls.

When the Foreshore Road was opened in 1877, the fair moved on to it, as did most of the "ball tossers", to the great annoyance of the local traders and business men.

After all this confusion a splendid new custom has started, that of the "kissing ring". Little is known of the rules of this game, and it was an instant success and a serious rival to the ball games. The "kissing ring" had a short life, because in 1982, it ceased. More than likely it was abolished on the grounds of being indecent and immoral.

There is nothing immoral in the Shrove Tuesday skipping at

Scarborough, in fact it is a "good time was had by all" sort of event, but how did it all start? There are a few theories put forward, but the most likely story is that the tradition arose from the time when all the fishermen used to go line fishing. The worst months for fishing were November, December and January, but the turning point for the fishermen coincides with Shrove Tuesday.

It was then that they stopped line fishing and used their boats for potting. Before going potting, the fishermen would sort through the ropes and would give the local children the rope that they were not going to use. As the years passed, this became an annual ritual, and after a period of time the children started to skip, and so it grew into what it is today, in that the whole town takes part.

On Shrove Tuesday 2001 a new tradition was started by the Scarborough Town Centre Management, who wanted the businesses and organisations to pick up their frying pans and take part in the first Pancake Day Olympics. The contestants were to take part in a relay race, and the Town Centre businesses showed a great interest in that Woolworths, Marks and Spencers, the Police, McDonalds, H.M.V., the Scarborough Building Society and many more – even the local Councillors gathered together two teams to take part.

The festivities are started by the Mayor of Scarborough ringing the "Pancake Bell" which at present is housed in the Rotunda Museum.

SKIPPING RHYMES

"Mother, mother, I feel sick,
Send for the doctor, quick, quick, quick.
Doctor, doctor. Shall I die?
Yes, my dear, and so shall I.
How many carriages shall I have?
One, two, three, four.

A rosy apple, a lemon or a tart,
Tell me the name of your sweetheart,
ABCDEFGHIJKLMNOPRSTUVWXYZ.
Will he marry me?
Yes, no, yes, no, yes, no, etc.
What will you go to the wedding in?
A wheelbarrow, an ass-and-cart,
A side-car, a motor-car, a gig, a hearse?
What kind of dress will you wear?
Silk, satin, cotton, velvet.
Voile, lustre, openwork, rags.
What kind of shoes will you wear?
Clogs, slippers, sandals,
High boots, low boots, button boots, shoes.

What kind of a house will you live in?
Country house, town house, city house, mud house,
Slate house, cement house, thatched house.
How many children will you have?
Om, two, three, four, five, etc.
What will he be when he grows up?
A tinker, a tailor, a soldier, a sailor,
A captain, a colonel, a cowboy, a thief,
A Lord, a Prince, a General, a Duke,
A Scotch Highlander . . .
Will he be drunk or sober?
(If "drunk")
Hit him with a poker, a poker, a poker.

Who goes boink?
A Kangaroo.
Who goes Gmrr?
A grizzly bear.

Who goes squeak?
A little brown mouse,
Who goes chitta-chatter, chitta chatter. chitta,
        chatter, chitta, chatter.

    I saw Esau sawing wood,
    And Esau saw I saw him;
    Though Esau saw I saw him saw
    Still Esau went an sawing.

    Monday night – the gramophone.
    Tuesday night we're all alone.
    Wednesday night I call the roll,
    Maureen, O Maureen,
    All the bays and all the girls
    They love bonny Maureen.

Charlie, Charlie, Chuck. Chuck, Chuck,
Went to bed with two old ducks,
One died, the other cried,
Charlie, Charlie, Chuck, Chuck, Chuck.

    A frog walked into a public house
    And asked for a pint of beer,
    Where's your money?
    In my pocket.
    Where's your pocket?
    I forgot it.
    Well, please walk out.

Teddybear, teddybear, touch the ground;
Teddybear, teddybear, turn right around,
Teddybear, teddybear, show your shoe,
Teddybear, teddybear, that will do:
Teddybear, teddybear, run upstairs,
Teddybear, teddybear, say your prayers;
Teddybear, teddybear, blow out the light,
Teddybear, teddybear, say good night,

Ice-cream, a penny a lump
The more you eat, the more you jump!
Eeper, Weeper. Chimney sweeper,
Married a wife and could not keep her.
Married another,
Did not love her,
Up the chimney he did shove her!

A hundrid an' ninety nine,
Me faither fell in the bine,
Ma mither caem oot wi' the washin' cloot
An skeipt his bare behind!

Waan toe three,
Ma mammy caught a flea;
She saltit it an'peppered it
An' pit it in hur tea.

The wind and the rain and the wind blew high
The rain comes blattering from the sky
(Anne Jane Murphy) says she'll die
If she doesn't get a fellow with a rolling eye.

She is handsome, she is pretty
She is the flower of Belfast City
She is courting, one, two, three,
Please could you tell me who is he?

Early in the morning at half-past eight
I heard the postman knocking at the gate
Postman, postman, drop your letter.
Lady, lady, pick it up,
I spy a lark, shining in the dark,
Echo. echo. G.O. stands for GO!

Julius Caesar,
The Roman Geezer,
Squashed his wife
With a lemon squeezer.

O, it's I have the tooth-ache,
A gumboil, a tummy-ache,
A pain on my left side
A pimple on my tongue
A hip, hip hurray!
To be the Queen of May
The Darkie says he'll marry her,
He'll marry her, marry her,
And take her out of the mill.
O we won't go home till morning
Till daybreak does appear. . .

Sam, Sam, the dirty man,
Washed his face in a frying pan,
He combed his hair with a donkey's tail,
And scratched his belly with a big toe nail.

(Albert Johnson) says he loves her
All the boys are dying for her
He raps at the window and he rings the bell
Saying, "My true lover, are you well?"

Out she comes as white as snow
With rings on her fingers and bells on each toe
And says to Albert with a sigh,
"I'm in love with a fellow with a rolling eye."

Strawberry, apple, my jamtart,
Tell me the name of your sweetheart,
A, B, C. D. E. F. G. H. I...

Pancake Bell and Curfew Bell

The custom of ringing a bell, either church or hand bell, on Pancake Tuesday, is still practised at a number of places in Yorkshire. It is an interesting local custom. Shrove Tuesday, which was the day in Roman Catholic times when people were shriven or absolved from sin (the bell calling them for this purpose), was a day of general rejoicing and liberation. The bell is usually rung at 11am, and at that time the schools would close for half a day and the apprentices left their work. The celebrations included the eating of food left in the house, and in particular pancakes. This was just before the long period of time of Lent, when everyone spent the time in prayer and abstinence.

BINGLEY: The Pancake Bell is rung by one of the church bell ringers at 11am on Shrove Tuesday.

RICHMOND: The Pancake Bell is rung at 11am on Shrove Tuesday to remind the womenfolk to prepare their pancakes to be consumed after this meal.

The Pancake Bell being rung at Bingley

165

The Curfew Bell is rung at eight o'clock in the evening every day. This is a survival from the days when the Conqueror ordered all fires to be raked out and covered. The bell is also rung every day at 8 o'clock in the morning, except Sunday, to arouse the drowsy.

SCARBOROUGH: Pancake Bell rung at midday. It used to be rung at St. Thomas the Martyr Hospital, but in 1861 the bell was moved to the Scarborough Museum. Since the late 1970's this bell has not been used due to a large crack in it, but the tradition has continued by ringing a ship's bell. The bell ringer receives a quarterly sum of 8 shillings.

The Pancake Bell being rung by the Mayor of Scarborough

ASCENSIONTIDE

The Penny Hedge of Horngarth

The legend of the Penny Hedge was originally taken from an ancient copy printed on vellum.

In the fifth year of the reign of King Henry II, three noblemen wer hunting a wild boar on Eskdaleside, near Whitby. The boar, being wounded and hotly pursued by the hounds, took refuge in the chapel and hermitage at Eskdaleside, which was then occupied by a monk from Whitby Abbey. The monk closed the door to keep out the hounds, and when the hunters came along they, in their anger, sent for the Abbot of Whitby who would have had them put to death. The monk, however, forgave them and said their lives should be spared "if they be content to be enjoyed to this penance, for the safeguard of their souls."

The penance is as follows:

You and yours shall hold your lands of the Abbot of Whitby, and his successors, in this manner: That upon Ascension Eve you, or some of you, shall come to the wood of Strayhead which is in Eskdaleside, the same day at Sunrising, and there shall the Officer of the Abbot blow his horn, to the intent that you may know how to find him, and he shall deliver unto you, William de Bruce, ten stakes, ten stout-stowers and ten Yedders, to be cut by you. Ralph de Piercie shall take one and twenty of each sort, to be cut in the same manner, and you Allatson shall take nine of each sort, to be cut as aforesaid, and to be taken on your backs, and carried to the town of Whitby: and so to be there before nine of the clock (if it is full sea, to cease service), as long as it is low water, at nine of the clock, the same hour each of you shall set your stakes at the edge of the water, each stake a yard from another, and so yedder them, so with yedders, and so stake on each side with your stout stowers that they stayed three tides without removing by the force of the water. Each of you shall make them in several places at the hour above named (except it be full sea at that hour, which, when it shall happen to pass, that services shall cease), and you shall do this service in remembrance that you did most cruelly slay me. And that you may the better call to God for Repentance, and find mercy, and do good works, the Officer of Eskdaleside shall blow his horn. Out on you, out on you, for the heinous crime of you. And if you and your successors do refuse this service, so long as it is not the full sea at that hour aforesaid, you and yours shall forfeit all their lands to the Abbot or his successors. Thus I do entreat the Abbot that you may have your lives and goods for this service, and you to promise to your Parts in Heaven, that it shall be done by you and your successors as it is afore-said.

The ancient horn is blown by the bailiff to the Lady of the Manor, who then cries, "Out on ye, out on ye".

This legend, according to tradition, took place on 16th October, 1159, but according to the terms of the penance, should it ever be made impossible by a "full sea" the duty need be performed no more. Until recently this had never been known to happen, but in 1981 it did happen, so the wrongdoers were absolved at last and the hermit could rest easy in his grave. He is of course responsible for a very quaint and enduring custom,

and instead of the custom ending because of the high sea in 1981, the present day owners of the land referred to in the hermit's will have continued with the building of the hedge for the benefit of the tourists.

What is the crowd who come along to watch the custom actually watching? As far back as 1770 a local Whitby historian declared that none of the characters in the story had actually existed, at least at the supposed time and under the names given to them by the legend. Nor was there a chapel on the site of the hermitage until nearly a hundred years after 1159. So how did the custom originate?

Some say that the hedge could have been a fish weir built at the beginning of the salmon fishing season. On the other hand, a structure of this nature is also called a Horngarth, which could have been a hedge or fence used to mark out the boundaries for the land cultivated by tenants of Whitby Abbey. The blowing of the horn each year could well have been the Abbot reminding the tenants that they were expected to make good any damage that had been done in the past year. When the practice fell out of favour, maybe an Abbot was not happy losing his rights as landlord, and the story of the hermit could well have been invented to justify the continuation of a custom that lent dignity to the ecclesiastical landlord. Why did the Monk (Abbot) choose Ascension Eve, which falls thirty-eight days after Easter? Could he have known that building a fence on this date meant that it would be very unlikely that the high tide could cause any difficulty, which meant that the custom would therefore have a long life.

OVER THE BORDER?

RUSH BEARING, SADDLEWORTH

Although Saddleworth is in Lancashire, the village was moved from Yorkshire in the great re-shuffle of counties in 1974. The people of Saddleworth were very upset with the decision, and even today they consider themselves as Yorkshire people, and not Lancastrians. Because of this great feeling it was felt that this Saddleworth custom should be included in this book.

The Saddleworth Rush Cart was ar one time, one of many such carts in the area, but now Saddleworth is on its own. (There were formerly carts at Cross, Boothurst, Friezeland, Harrop Dale, Burnedge, Uppermill and Greenfield.) The rush cart comes out on the second Saturday and Sunday in August.

The rush cart has two or four wheels, and on it is built a four-sided tower of rushes that have been collected from local rush fields.

The front of the tower is decorated with a piece of cloth, usually with the year, and Saddleworth Rush Cart painted on it. The cart is pulled by the Saddleworth Morris Men holding staves attached to a long pole known as a "stang" and is pulled round the surrounding villages. Having got round all the pubs en route, they then give a dance display for the villagers.

There are around 40 men pulling the "stang", with others at the back of the cart to act as a brake.

This very active custom was revived in 1975, and has been getting better and bigger every year. There are a few rules that the Morris Men have to comply with before becoming a fully-fledged member:

If a MorrisMan drops his stick, he has to buy a drink for all the man.

Before he is allowed to wear a waistcoat, he has to dance at the Rood

*1975 Rush Cart proceeding through Delph village
led by Harold Buckley, veteran rushcarter*

End Fair on Maundy Thursday.

All new members must drink a yard of ale.

If a lady touches the cart, she will be pregnant within twelve months. This has been proven true, many times.

A man sits astride the rush tower, and by tradition, he has to drink a pint of ale at every pub stop.

There are other activities going on including wrestling – on a 1 in 2 hillside – gurning, which entails making horrible faces through a horse collar.

What a weekend – it must be seen to be believed!

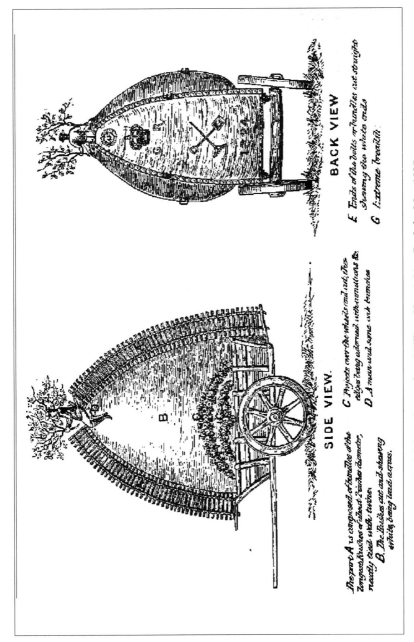

Rochdale rush cart, from William Hone's Year Book for May 1825

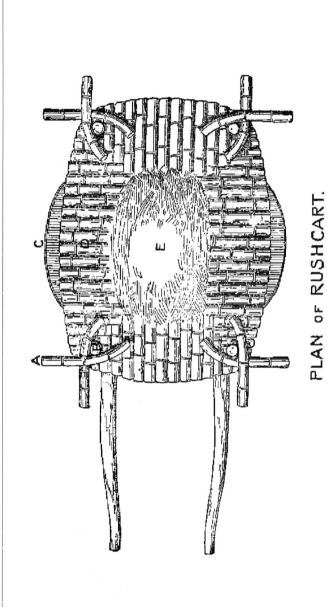

PLAN OF RUSHCART.

A. The edges of "feather wings" formed of small bundles of rushes about 2 inches thick.
B. Reds set up in the angles to give shape and strength.
C. Line of feathering over the wheel.
D. Longitudinal lines of rushes the tier being smoothly cut.
E. Loose rushes to fill up the cart, will tie the wheel down.

Rochdale rush cart, from William Hone's Year Book for May 1825

INDEX